JEWISH FATHERS
A Legacy of Love

JEWISH FATHERS
A Legacy of Love

Photographs by Lloyd Wolf

Interviews by Paula Wolfson

Foreword by Rabbi Harold Kushner

VERVE
EDITIONS

For People of All Faiths, All Backgrounds

JEWISH LIGHTS Publishing
Woodstock, Vermont

I dedicate this book to my parents, Eric and Elicia Wolf, to my daughter, Emma Sky Wolf, to my brother, Dean Wolf, to Dion Johnson, Regina Porter, and Jazmin and Justin Johnson. May your lives be filled with peace and blessings. —Lloyd Wolf

To my father, Harry Wolfson, a World War II veteran, a labor and union activist, and the first Jewish comedian I ever met. And to my sister, Ellen, and her partner, Kathleen Fallon, for their compassionate caretaking efforts. —Paula Wolfson

ACKNOWLEDGMENTS

Lloyd Wolf ~ Paula Wolfson

Many people were generous to us with their time, suggestions, and ideas in the process of making this book, opening their hearts, minds, and in many cases, their homes. We would like to thank you all. It is deeply appreciated.

Gary Chassman of Verve Editions whose energies and expertise were critical in bringing this work to fruition, Jeff Rubin for his advice and early support, our extraordinary tri-lingual transcriber and scholar, Dorothy Schwalb, Paul Brown, Gary and Kit Putnam and the excellent staff at Black and White Lab—especially Sean Carroll, our book designer Stacey Hood, Stacey Freed, Eric Rozenmann, Stephanie Gross, Kenneth Grant, Dean Wolf, Ronda Robinson, Frank London, Tine Kindermann, Dr. Suzanne Schuweiler-Daab, Leslie Stone, David Hafner, Theresa Moorleghan, Glen Thornton, Kevin and Bette Breen, Miriam Isaacs, Nurite Notarius-Rosin, Kerry Miskin, Barbara Golumb, Matt and Elizabeth Portnoy, Gail Prensky, Becky O'Brien, Barbara Gould, Marcia and Howard Fine, Herb and Jean Nalibow, Steven Unger, Margaret Cook, Wendy Talbert, Rabbi Avi Magid, Lisa Falk, Lynn Zuckerkorn, Lynne Halevi, Betsy Staller, Carol Grosman, Sherry Rose, Trudy Wong, Fran Eizenstat, Deborah and Mike Warshowsky, Virginia Spatz, Kent Kiser, Jim Zachar, Mary Gratch, Tara Andringa, Kathleen Long, Toby and Norman Levi, Jacki Rosen, Susana Flaum, Dr. Joyce Antler, Carol and Cliff Krause and family, Caroline Keene, Yaakov and Resna Hammer, Rhoda Wolfson, Ellen Wolfson, Syd Lemmerman, Susan Weidman Schneider, Howard Bragman, Lynne Rosenstein, Jonathan Falk, Rabbi Lisa Edwards, Peter Deer, Sheila Gaisin, Ruth Heller, Esther Siegel, Gail Shirazi, Samy Ymar, Rachel Maryn, Judybeth Greene, Philip Brookman, Amy Brookman, Andy Silow-Carrol, Carolyn Hessel, Mary Candel, Judith Sokolow, Sherri Waas Shunfenthal, Ruth Friedman, Judi Rosenzweig, Ronnie and Marc Katz, Laura Kruger, Jonathan Friedlander, Mimi Xang Ho, Jean Bloch Rosensaft, Menachem Rosensaft, Aida Wasserstein, Debbie Nussbaum, Mark Rubin, Deborah Boteach, Hedda Kopf, Marcia Diamond, Emily Sprissler, Beverly Chalifoux, Robin Jackson, Hilary Lehman, Allison Silberberg, Arlene Stein, Joel and Ellie Bluestein, Michael Warshow, Elaine Schonberger, Nancy Cohen, Alex and Cindy Cohn, Scott Pelligrino, Melanie Rich, Ronnie Van Gelder, Sandy Berman, Fran Kaplan, Barbara Christopher, Maureen and David Meadows, Amy Arno Smith, Linda Haase, Amy Terkel, my photo-documentary students at George Mason University, and the hidden lamed-vovniks who helped us find our way.

We also wish to express our appreciation to the wonderful men who gave of their time and opened their lives to us, but whose stories we were not able to include in the final version of the book: Brian Cahen, Larry Cohler, Chaim Fruchter, John Golumb, Merv Lemmerman, Joe Reiswerg, Tank Rubinette, Louis Shemaria, Judah Siegel, Mike Tabor, and Harry Wolfson.

CONTENTS

FOREWORD

Rabbi Harold Kushner

Becoming a father will rarely have the power to redefine a man's life to the extent that becoming a mother will redefine a woman's. Its physical impact is significantly less and its emotional impact will usually be less as well. We too often read of fathers walking away from the responsibilities of fatherhood while women will rarely abdicate the responsibilities of motherhood.

And yet the experience of becoming a father can say so much to a man about what it means to be a man and, for that matter, what it means to be a human being.

"And Enoch walked with God after the birth of his son." (Genesis 5:22) To father a child is, in a way, to partake of the divine, to bring a new soul into the world even as God did in the first days of Creation, to cheat mortality by seeing to it that your name and your values, as well as your DNA, will survive your limited time on earth.

To be a Jewish father is to locate yourself in a chain of tradition, a chain of generations stretching back to the day when a band of newly liberated slaves stood at Sinai and agreed to pledge their newly won freedom to the service of God, and to transmit that commitment to their children. To be a Jewish father is to say "as my father entrusted a tradition to me, I now accept the obligation to pass it on to my child." And these words that I command you today shall be in your heart. You shall teach them diligently to your children." (Deut. 6:6-7)

To be a Jewish father is to inherit the obligation to teach

Aron and Elaine Lichtman

not only your own children but to teach the society around you what it means to be a man. Interestingly, Judaism, which distinguishes so sharply between the religious roles of men and those of women, has traditionally guided men to let the feminine side of their soul emerge. In Erich Fromm's typology of mother love ("You are bone of my bone and flesh of my flesh and nothing you ever do will make me stop loving you.") and father love ("I will love you if you earn my love."), Jewish fathers traditionally embraced their sons and daughters with both kinds of love. Where some gentile fathers would tell their sons to "be a man," many Jewish fathers would tell their sons to "be a mensch." Jewish fathers were role models of piety, fidelity, and learning, not only competitiveness and achievement, as emblems of manliness.

Jewish daughters need Jewish fathers to assure them that they are loveable and give them the confidence to go forth into a world that will often judge them by irrelevant factors.

Jewish sons need Jewish fathers to teach them to be a mensch and not buy into the notions of manliness so often purveyed by American culture.

And more than anything, the world, a world too ready to resort to anger and violence, needs the examples of good Jewish fathers to show it a more humane way of being manly.

In this book, we are pleased to introduce you to a variety of Jewish fathers, as men remember their fathers and contemplate their relationship to their own children. ■

Lloyd Wolf ~ Paula Wolfson

Family matters. Fathers matter. No book of this type has yet been created exploring and honoring the role of contemporary American Jewish fathers. The father's critical role in family life has been under-reported. We have gathered the stories of a diverse and representative cross-section of American Jewish men. They tell in their own words how they meet the challenges of parenting, and the photographs provide a window of insight into their world. The work complements and completes the circle begun with our book *Jewish Mothers: Strength, Compassion, Wisdom.* As Eric Wolf, the photographer's father put it, "it's our turn." We have now come full circle.

This book is our way of acknowledging and paying tribute to the success story of Jewish fathers in America. At the turn of the twentieth century the majority of Eastern European Jewish immigrants arrived on Ellis Island impoverished and unable to speak English. Now, at the beginning of the 21st century, we can mark how far we have come. There are those who feel that the golden age of Judaism in America is now. Many Jews have succeeded beyond the dreams of their struggling and oppressed ancestors. Within the United States, anti-Semitic acts and hate crimes no longer dominate American Jewish news. Despite differences of opinion about specific policies, there has been continuing support for Israel's existence from most walks of American life. America has been immeasurably enriched by its Jewish citizens. Jews have served on the Supreme Court, in Congress, and as Cabinet Secretaries. Senator Joseph Lieberman began his speech at the 2000 Democratic Convention for the vice presidency by saying that he wished his father had lived to see the day. Jewish policemen walk the beat in New York City. Jewish scientists regularly win Nobel Prizes. Many Jewish fathers have contributed to the stability of the family in America and in every field of endeavor—from Dr. Seuss to Dr. Jonas Salk, George Gershwin to Chaim Potok, Hank Greenberg, Steven Spielberg, Felix Frankfurter, Rabbi Abraham Joshua Heschel, Ben Shahn, Robert Oppenheimer, Admiral Hyman Rickover, the Marx Brothers: the list goes on and on. However, in this book we have been most focused not on the notables, but on the day-to-day heroism, challenges, and accomplishments of the Jewish men who modestly go about raising their families and quietly contributing to our society. You. Your brother. Your father.

In Yiddish, the image of the Jewish father is synonymous with "mensch," a good person. The word mensch is used by both Jews and non-Jews and has become part of America's vocabulary.

The first mensch we meet in life is usually our father.

Hardworking. Honest. Kind. Fair. Reliable. Charitable. Funny. Reverent. Mature. Honorable. Sturdy. Learned. Righteous. Modest. Responsible. The man in your temple who quietly gives to charity. The coach of your kid's soccer team. The nice guy you hope your sister will hook up with. A mensch.

In Yiddish mensch literally means "man" or the "quality of being male." However, it implies all the qualities of what it takes to be an upright, trustworthy person. Perhaps the greatest compliment that can be paid to a Jew is to refer to him (or her) as a mensch. Being a mensch has nothing to do with status or wealth. It is a word that is used democratically, employed to describe a kindergarten teacher, a shopkeeper, or a Little League coach in the same vein as a noted philanthropist, a preeminent scientist, or even a senator. It levels people on the basis of their conduct, not on their fame. It is a standard to be lived up to, a standard that Jewish fathers have been charged with since the times of the Biblical Patriarchs, Abraham, Isaac, and Jacob.

The first Jew, Abraham, is often referred to as Avraham Avinu, "Abraham Our Father," the father of the Jewish people. Abraham had the first vision of God, and it was with Abraham that God made the covenant, his eternal promise. But Abraham did not have children until he was very old. His first son was Ishmael, born to his concubine, Hagar. Abraham was 100 when he had his son Isaac by his wife, Sarah. Responding to the word of God, a distressed Abraham listened to his wife's wishes and exiled Hagar and Ishmael (the ancestor of the Arabs) into the desert. Abraham was consoled by God's promise that Ishmael would also be the father of a great nation.

In Genesis 22, God tests Abraham, demanding that he take his son Isaac, now a grown man, and sacrifice him. He lashes Isaac onto an altar of wood and stone. As Abraham raises his knife to kill his son, an angel speaks from heaven and commands him not to harm Isaac, informing Abraham that he has met God's test. A ram is offered up for slaughter instead. After Sarah's death, Abraham remarries and has six children by Keturah. Isaac and Abraham are never mentioned together again until Abraham's death, where Isaac and his estranged brother, Ishmael, come together to bury their father.

It's a complex and richly human tale, presenting many tangled issues. Foremost is the question of what kind of father, listening to the voice of a deity that only he can hear, would obey a command to kill his child. It's a haunting example of behavior for those of us with very real sons and daughters. Yet the Torah consistently presents Abraham as a righteous man, a peaceful visionary, blessed and informed by God in every way. Among other things, it lets us know that our great role models were at times unfathomable and imperfect human beings, not demigods, and that parenthood involves difficult choices and faith.

Inseparable from man's covenant with God is the belief that the descendants of Abraham are a "chosen people." The children of Israel stand in a unique relationship to God. It is a relationship that, like father and child, is continually tested. Because man is made in the image of God (b'tselem Elohim) and has free will, he is able to choose between acts of good or evil. This is the essential struggle of all humanity in every generation.

There are other fascinating father-child stories in the Bible. Joseph, the son shipped into slavery who rose to become Pharoah's chief advisor, has a dramatic reunion with his own father, the patriarch Jacob. To this day Jewish boys are blessed in the name of Joseph's sons, Ephraim and Menasheh. Moses, our greatest teacher and leader of the Exodus from slavery, has no notable children—they are mentioned only in passing. The sons of Aaron, the first High Priest, are killed by an act of God for their presentation of "strange fire" before the holy tabernacle. Later, King Saul alienates his son Jonathan who has befriended Saul's rival, the future King David. David's son, King Solomon the Wise, fulfills his father's dream by building the Temple in Jerusalem. The original Twelve Tribes of Israel were headed by the twelve sons of Jacob. And the light of Judaism was kept burning by Judah Maccabee and his brothers at the prompting and leadership of their father, Mattityahu, ending in the miracle celebrated each year at Chanukah.

The Talmud teaches that "a father has the following obligations towards his son—to circumcise him, to redeem him if he is a firstborn (pidyon haben), to teach him Torah, to find him a wife, and to teach him a craft or a trade. And there are some who say that he must also teach him how to swim." (Babylon Talmud, Kiddushin 29a)

Most American Jewish men become fathers and are actively involved in their children's lives. Family is the central concern in their personal lives but it is rarely acknowledged publicly. The daily act of raising children is seldom affirmed. Most fathers are too busy to stop and reflect on this role and are trained not to make a big fuss over it. Nonetheless, fathers are critical to the healthy development of children, as has been indicated in numerous studies. This fact in no way denigrates the role and influence of mothers nor should it be used to make the task of single parents more burdensome. Women, both traditionally and in con-temporary practice, have shouldered much of the daily responsibilities for childrearing.

Larry Cohler and Ayelet Cohler-Esses

Yet in most families, men create a foundation and model for their sons and daughters that is significant in their basic upbringing. Different fathers have vastly differing approaches to parenting: in how they discipline, in how they teach their children, and in what values they hope to impart in the division of labor between mother and father both within the home and in the workplace.

We have examined issues facing all types of fathers in modern American society from a Jewish perspective. There are numerous challenges facing contemporary American Jewish fathers. Issues of balancing career and family responsibilities, intermarriage and assimilation, education, single parenting, gender-identity issues, education, special challenges (raising children with special needs), divorce and custody questions, step-parenting, discipline, ethnic identity, and religious observance. There are concerns about declining family size among the non-Orthodox (a noted rabbi has quipped that "the most effective form of birth control in the American Jewish community is graduate school"), economic pressures, consumer culture, and changes in traditional family roles. Fostering Jewish identity in a free society like America is largely a new experience in Jewish history. The existence of the State of Israel and its ongoing troubles also presents fathers with identity issues for themselves and their children. Still, after surviving millennia of far more formidable obstacles, we are likely to pass on our legacy to succeeding generations with creativity, energy, and continually renewed hope.

A nearly universal observation about these men is that they both learned and taught by example. They observed their father's life and actions as a model for their own positive behaviors, though in some cases they spoke about behaviors they chose not to emulate. Interestingly, these men were more comfortable speaking on record of negative roles their fathers played in their lives than were the women we profiled in our book *Jewish Mothers*. Hard work, integrity, and honesty were principal among the values they learned from their fathers and hoped to pass on as a legacy to their children. Almost all stated that they wanted their children to be happy, self-sufficient, and to be able to enjoy life. While many spoke about education and tikkun olam (doing works of charity and healing) as being important, they did not emphasize them as prominently in their system of values as we observed in American Jewish women. Perhaps the balance of both parents' natural emphases—on education, enjoying life, acts of charity, hard work, integrity, and self-sufficiency—have been the ingredients for both the individual and collective success of Jews in this country.

Several of our older subjects observed that they were more hands-on as grandparents than they had been as fathers. In general there was more of a division of labor between the sexes in childrearing when they were young parents than there is today. Their wives took care of the kids while they knocked themselves out making a living for the family. Some expressed regrets about this, but more expressed admiration and devotion—and greatly credited—their wives' work in direct childcare. This hands-off parenting was certainly not universal, as exemplified by the narratives we heard from Rabbi Morris Goldfarb and Sam Heller. The majority of younger men spoke naturally about trying to be equal partners with their wives in both childcare and in making a living. Many insisted on mentioning their partnerships with their wives or their wives' contributions.

Dr. Lawrence Fuchs, professor emeritus at Brandeis University, makes the observation in his book *Beyond Patriarchy: Jewish Fathers and Families,* that Judaism was the first and only ancient culture to moderate the power of male patriarchy. While he argues that patriarchy has always existed (and makes no excuses for its inequities), the fact is that even in antiquity Jewish men forged a partnership with the women in the community. They accorded them rights and status far beyond any other culture on the planet. There are numerous examples of this beginning as far back as the Torah: the vaunted status of the Matriarchs, the right to negotiate for themselves and own property (the daughters of Zelophehad), the inclusion of mothers in the Ten Commandments, women's roles in society as prophetesses and judges (Miriam and Deborah), the ode "Eyshet Chayil" (Woman of Valor) in Proverbs, among many others. This had obvious and powerful ramifications for individual families and for the fundamental success and nature of Jewish life.

Is there a specific style of Jewish fathering? This is a difficult question to answer, but there are some common themes and histories. Jewish men certainly have a generally good reputation in America as making good husbands and fathers (though as one interview subject joked, "Now, if only Jewish women would say that, it would be great."). This reputation comes from both tradition and practice. It can be argued that the Jewish community is one of the most successful immigrant groups in America. We believe that the reasons for this come from basic structures and values fostered within most Jewish families.

Family is a central focus of Judaism. The role of the father has been crucial. In the long years of exile, Jewish fathers provided for their families in difficult and often brutally adverse situations. Ethical conduct, learning, faith, hard work, and the integrity of family were the mainstays of continuity, of the heritage passed from fathers to their children. The great role models in Judaism have always been scholars, philanthropists, communal leaders, upright businessmen: mensches, not warriors or strongmen. Strength is to come from applied wisdom and righteous living, not merely through the application of blunt force. Traditional Jewish values are of civilization, not of the jungle.

In doing this book, we have tried to be as inclusive as possible within the American Jewish community. We crisscrossed the country, from the waters of Cape Cod to Hawaiian beaches, sunny Los Angeles to a bris in Brooklyn, the snows of Colorado to the august halls of the U.S. Senate, a South Carolina front porch to an airplane hangar in Oklahoma. We heard music played on the streets of the Lower East Side of Manhattan and in a quiet backyard in Virginia. Our travels brought us to the NBA All-Star game in Philadelphia, a Little League field in Florida, a world-famous delicatessen (try the blintzes at the Carnegie Deli. They're worth the heart attack. Trust us.), a police station, a book illustrator's studio, and a daycare center in Texas. We sat in lots of living rooms and kitchens where we were treated with kindness, listening to men sharing their intimate moments, the songs of their lives and hearts. The men profiled are young, old, married, single, straight, gay, Reform, Conservative, Orthodox, Chasidic, unaffiliated, secular, immigrants, native-born, and converts. They are adoptive fathers, wealthy, financially struggling, rural, urban, veterans, doctors, attorneys, media professionals, educators, rabbis, Holocaust survivors, philanthropists, businessmen, engineers, homeschoolers, stay-at-home dads,

David and Miranda Frum

politicians, artists, athletes, and "Vermont's only shomer-Shabbes, organic, kosher, horsepowered maple sugar farmer." We found them all articulate, fascinating, committed, and dedicated to their kids. Our only regret is that the book couldn't be longer, to include all of the truly fine men we met with and heard about. We hope that you will recognize something here of your own father, partner, brother, uncle, son—or yourself—and reflect on their story and important contributions to your life.

So, sit down with your own father, ask him about his life, and listen closely. As Eric Wolf put it, "Just because I don't show my emotions, it doesn't mean I don't have them." We guarantee that your father will appreciate it and you'll probably learn something meaningful in the process. And if you're lucky, he might pick up the tab for dinner.

Family matters. Fathers matter. ■

Gad Alon of Portland, Oregon was born in Israel in 1949 and relocated with his family to the United States in 1963. He is the program chairperson of Clinton School, working with students who experience emotional disturbance, learning problems, and behavior challenges. He was part of a team that founded the school in 1976. Gad has also found a creative outlet of expression and is experimenting with becoming an artist. He and his wife, Barbara, have two children, Bati and Ori.

GAD ALON

Becoming a father has been the most important experience of my life. Fatherhood is a profound journey of learning. I always had both fantasies and fears about having children. There were no good role models in my family. I really felt like I was going into it blindly. When Barbara was pregnant with Bati, the entire experience was romantic; I felt I was joining some ancient fraternity of readiness and maturity. At the same time, I was terrified—the permanance of this commitment was daunting. I also felt as if I were the first person to ever have a child; my excitement seemed unparalleled. I wondered if these feelings were the beginning of the preparation process for becoming a parent, both for the difficult and joyous times to come.

My own father, though a loving man, did not receive the gift of having been parented by his father. His parents died in Germany when he was young and he and his brothers were raised by a friend of the family. I think he became very insecure when my sister and I were born, having to confront his own lack of knowledge or instinct in being a father. This also manifested in the way he chose to raise us as Jews. His own Jewish upbringing was halted when his parents died, as the family that raised him was Christian. In my home, growing up, we celebrated few modern Jewish holidays, none of which had a religious focus. The legacy of this family history and my experience as a secular Jew in Israel contributed to the ongoing exploration of my own Judaism.

When Bati was born, this exploration took a new turn as I began questioning my own Jewish practices and if or how I was going to pass some of them to her. Since I am an atheist, the question of raising my children as Jews was an issue I had to confront very seriously. While Judaism did not feel like a religion to me, it did feel like a culture into which I was born and one I appreciated and loved very much. It was a part of my soul, my skin and bones, my way of thinking and my identification. How could I not pass that on to my children? We gave both of our children Hebrew names. Batya, means "daughter of god" and Bati means "I have arrived" and she did, directly into my hands. I caught her right out of the womb. It was so beautiful, an amazing experience and I knew that we had an instant connection. My son Ori's name means "my light." He is full of love and lights up my life. It felt natural to give them these names, not just because of their relevant meaning, but because it helped connect them to a place and history within them. I spoke Hebrew to both of the children when they were little and began to light Shabbat candles on Friday nights. I told them stories from the Old Testament and read about upcoming holidays. While we practice these fairly traditional Jewish rituals, I am honest with the children about my lack of belief in god, and don't include god's name when saying the prayers.

As the children grew we began to think about how to further incorporate Judaism into our lives. Eventually, we joined a reconstructionist synagogue, Havurah Shalom, and began to attend a variety of holidays, functions, and activities. While I do have some ambivalence about the religious focus of some of these activities, I feel wonderful about the Jewish community we have developed in our family's life. I have had to accept that being a Jew in America is not like being a Jew in Israel, where Judaism is a part of everyday life. In America, there must be an intention in creating awareness of one's own Judaism. I am committed to exposing my children to a variety of Jewish practices and allowing a natural process for them to determine their own commitment to who they will become as Jews.

Now I do all the household stuff with the kids. I bathe them and read to them almost every night. We don't do television in this house. I also tend to be very adventurous. Before the kids came Barb and I made a vow not to stop our travels. When Bati was only six weeks old we took her sailing in the Greek Islands. This is her legacy now. Bati knows that she is a traveler.

I'm hoping that my children know themselves well so that when tough decisions come, they're able to struggle through them and not feel regrets. I want them to have that strength early in their life. Because I work with emotionally disturbed teenagers I really feel very comfortable about the idea of my children becoming teens. Yet, I know it will be a challenge and that you can't protect your kids from the world.

Just hearing them say, "Papa I love you" makes it all OK. ■

Sam Bloch of Rego Park, New York, was a partisan fighting in the forests of Russia in World War II. He was director of The Herzl Press, is the senior vice president of the American Gathering of Holocaust Survivors, is active in the World Jewish Restitution Organization, and is chairman of the American Friends of the Diaspora Museum in Tel Aviv. He has two children, Jean and Gloria.

SAM BLOCH

I was born in a little town called Ivye in what is today Belarus. My father devoted his life to Hebrew education. Passover was a joyous observance in our house. My father used to conduct the Seder. He taught me a lot of songs. He was a modern Orthodox man, no beard, no peyes, no black hat. But Shabbat was Shabbat. He subscribed to a Hebrew newspaper from Warsaw. He called me in one day, and said, "I want you to read this." The headline was "The Eternal Hatred For The Eternal People." He said, "I don't know what fate has in store for us in the future."

In September 1939 our area was occupied by the invading Russian army. They closed all the Hebrew schools. Father lost his position because of the Communist anti-Zionist campaign. I stayed with an aunt and got my Russian education. I graduated on June 20, 1941. That was a day of panic because there were mass arrests of Jews by the the Soviets. I was sure my parents were going to be deported. I rushed home. All of a sudden bombs started flying. A Nazi bomb fell into our garden, ripped off the roof of our house, beginning the German attack.

We left to a village for a few days. An order came from the German command that all the men should report to the marketplace. I did not go. My father couldn't hide because he was known and they took him away. They selected 220 people, the Jewish intelligencia. They locked them up with beatings and screamings. A truck would take out 20 or 25 of them and drive them away. At 17 I found myself at the head of the family with responsibility for my mother and little brother.

A peasant with rags around his feet said to me, "You idiot Jews, you believe the Germans, that they took away the people deep into Poland? I saw what happened. I live on a farm overlooking the forest. They brought the Jews there, forced them to dig a grave and shot them all." We went where he said, started digging and found bodies. I did not find my father, but found others from the group, all shot in the head. We said Kaddish on the spot. There was no crying. I came home and said to mother, "Papa will never come back. He's dead. We cannot trust the Germans. We'll survive together."

May 12th was the big killing, 3,500 people. When the SS came to chase us out of the house we were in our hiding place. We heard shooting and screaming outside. Then deadly silence fell. We deliberated what we were going to do. We had a Polish maid, Sonya, who lived about 15 kilometers away in a village. We'd go there. After three days we went out. We put my mother and my brother in an empty coffin. I wore a yellow badge, as though I was a local Jewish policeman accompanying the coffin. That's how we snuck out.

A Jewish ghetto was established behind a barbed wire fence. I was working in a drugstore. One day, a man comes in, a German officer, Helmut Himmelstass. He said, "Do you know how to make eggnog?" Three times a week he would fill up bottles and drink with his cronies. He used to escort me to the ghetto gate. I got packets full of food; meat, milk, bread, medicines. The Polish local police were afraid to touch me because I was escorted by a Nazi! He started talking politics, "I am a member of the Nazi party except on one point. What Hitler is doing to the Jews is a crime against our own people." He had witnessed the killings and said, "I am ashamed to be a German."

We started organizing an underground in the ghetto. We acquired arms and dug a tunnel. The operative plan was, if they come to get us, sound an alarm, and escape.

The German officer pulled me aside one day and started hitting me. He wanted to bring me to my senses. He said, "The Jews are letting yourselves be killed like dogs. The Nazi high commissioner told us that by the end of 1942 the entire area will be rid of all Jews. I know that the old and the children have no chance to survive. If you want to rebuild your people, where is your youth?" He did not know that we already had an underground organization. I asked him, "Where should we go?" He shouted, "Go to the forest. The trees and the birds will teach you to survive."

The choice was to leave my mother and brother and escape. I vowed to stay together or die together. One evening a man knocked on our window. He was a religious Catholic, Bernard, very poor. He said to mother, "Your husband saved my life in the First World War. I had a dream and one of the saints told me, 'you owe a debt to Mrs. Bloch.' The saint gave me orders to rescue you."

Fifteen people were hiding in the room, and everybody heard. My mother said, "What am I going to do about the others?" He said, "I'll take everybody. There's another farmer, Stom. He will make room in his pigsty." After the liquidation of

the Ivye ghetto we fled to his farm. He used to bring us a few potatoes. He brought us the newspaper from which we learned about the defeat of the German Army in Stalingrad. Even though we were full of lice, we saw the first rays of hope.

Our farmer got pneumonia, the priest came for confession. Two days later, he was dead. His wife Marilla came and said, "I'll keep you till the end of the war." About ten days later she didn't bring us food. I saw through the cracks, again the priest is coming. Marilla is dead. A couple of days later somebody opens the lock on our barn door, whispering "Jews, where are you?" The new owner warned, "Everybody knows you are here! Whoever acts against God's will and saves Jews gets punished. If you don't leave tomorrow, I am going to the SS and hand you over."

All of a sudden…horses, and shouts! We assumed this was the end. Somebody opened the barn doors and yelled in Yiddish "Jews! Come out!" I saw my friends from the underground. They came in full force to get us. We were dirty and emaciated and here were these boys with red cheeks, bullets, machine guns, and rifles! We went to the forest and settled in their bunker. There were 1200 Jews. Women, children, fighting men in the forest, 500 miles behind German lines.

We went on missions to plant bombs under railroad tracks. Some of my friends had TNT to blow up a German train. They were caught by a Russian group who took away the explosives, confiscated their arms and boots, just because they were Jews. We had troubles not only from Germans, but also from Russians. There were decent Russians too.

We were liberated at the end of June 1944. The last day was very tense, because the Germans stumbled onto our camp and started shooting. We alerted Russian army groups and they killed many Germans. Some Jews wanted revenge. We took three SS officers prisoner and found pictures of them shooting Jews. An old man, Avigdor, took a knife. He went to one of the Germans, cut off pieces of his ear saying, "This is for my daughter, Sarah, this is for my son, Yitzchak." Nobody stopped him.

I returned to my hometown, my mother and brother in hand. Our house was occupied by strangers. We realized it would be impossible for us to rebuild our life, every stone was full of Jewish blood. We applied for exit permits and went to Lodz, Poland. There were a lot of Jews there, survivors from the camps, partisans, and Zionists. I joined the clandestine Bricha organization and smuggled thousands onto the illegal boats to Palestine.

There was a knock on my door. "The Russian police are after you. Take the train to Stettin. At the railroad station, you'll see a man with a red handkerchief. This is our agent." We left quickly, met the agent and were put on a truck to Berlin. We got arrested by Russian military police. They took me twice a week, blindfolded, for interrogation about the Jewish underground. I stuck to my story: "We are thankful to the Russians for liberating us. I want to reach Bergen Belsen to find my father, who has, supposedly, survived." I did not betray anything.

I volunteered to clean the commandant's office. He had a piano. The captain asked "You know Russian war songs?" I played him a song about a Russian mother. He gave me cards, a bottle of wine, chocolates. One day, I saw a German packing books. I asked him to take a letter to 'Arthur' the code name for an agent from Palestine. It worked. One morning my officer said, "Tomorrow you're going to your homeland." I thought I would die. Outsmarting the Germans, outsmarting the Russians, and at the very end I get sent to Siberia. He laughed, "We have orders from Stalin to free you."

I got a passport and left for the Bergen Belsen refugee camp. I got involved helping the illegal immigration to Israel, smuggling arms to Palestine. We began to feel life coming back into us out of the ashes. Two thousand kids were born in Bergen Belsen. One day, I saw a beautiful girl. She and her parents had survived hidden under a floor by a farmer. I was impressed that she was studying medicine at the University of Bonn. Because of her, I also registered there. I took up political science and international law. Then her parents got affidavits to go to America. I tried to persuade them to go to Palestine. It didn't work out, so we got married by a rabbi in Bergen Belsen.

I made it to the U.S.A. with my mother and my brother. I started working for the Jewish Agency and became the director of their publishing program. Jeanie was our first child, then came Gloria. I never made it a business of teaching my daughters about what had happened to us, but whenever we had a gathering of survivors we took them along. They established the International Network Of Children Of Holocaust Survivors. We have a responsibility to imbue the second generation with a sense of memory because 20 years from now there will be no survivors. Somebody should continue it. We are very proud of our children who do their share in acts of remembrance. ■

Dr. Lawrence Fuchs of Canton, Massachusetts, Brandeis University Professor Emeritus, the author of Beyond Patriarchy: Jewish Fathers and Families, The Political Behavior of American Jews, *was the first director of the Peace Corps in the Philippines, and vice chairman of the U.S. Commission on Immigration Reform.*

DR. LAWRENCE FUCHS

I love being a father and teacher. It must have to do with immortality and the joy of having another human being with whom you feel a connection. And there is the sheer fun of watching children and grandchildren.

I have tried to teach my children universal values inherent in Judaism. I authored a book on Judaism and patriarchy. The movement towards equality between men and women begins with the Jewish story. The only ancient culture that modified male-domination significantly was Judaism. Torah's view on women is that they are children of HaShem and should be given rights. Although some feminists may disagree, there is acknowledgment in Torah of the economic and sexual rights of females and the responsibility of fathers for children. Torah instructs fathers to teach sons moral values and to consult their wives on family decisions. This is strikingly different from other ancient civilizations.

My grandfather came from Poland to escape anti-Semitism. He moved with his wife and my father, then nine, into an impoverished neighborhood on the Lower East Side. My grandfather became ill so my father left school and became responsible for the family. Father was a fur broker known for his integrity. He was not much involved as a father, but was an honest and responsible man. But he was not an easy man to be married to or be the son of. He was intolerant of foibles and stupidities. I didn't learn the beauty of Judaism from him, but absorbed his responsibility, generosity, and honesty. We reacted to how we were raised. Father never picked up a dishcloth. I'll never forget the day my brother said to me, "Let's do the dishes. Mom works too hard."

I grew up in a cookie-cutter apartment building, mostly Jewish. Upwardly mobile. Small businessmen. Worked hard. Mothers tried to dress their kids properly and made sure that they behaved, went to school, and were healthy. It was not an intellectual world. It was a world of young American Jews striving to make it. Families donated money to charity and to Israel, but the goal was to go into business.

I made use of the GI bill and went to college. I observed the professors and thought, "They talk about what they're reading and thinking. That's good." You work hard, but you're more the owner of your time than in most jobs. While in college I married and began my family.

I want to teach what I know about Judaism to my children and grandchildren. I wrote something for them, *A Grandfather Answers Questions about Jews and Judaism.* I want them to embrace the presence and blessings of HaShem and to understand the history and culture of the Jews.

Sen. Carl Levin (D Michigan) has chaired the Senate Armed Services Committee and serves on the Government Affairs Committee, and the Senate Select Committee on Intelligence. He and his wife, Barbara, have three daughters and three grandchildren. His brother, Sander Levin, is a U.S. Congressman from Michigan.

SENATOR CARL LEVIN

My father was a compassionate person who believed in listening to other people's opinions, including his children's. He made us feel as though what we had to say was important. We would never eat dinner without my father and that was when he discussed politics with us. My father was a New Dealer, a big supporter of FDR. He had a tremendous social conscience and represented farm workers free, during the 1930s when nobody else was interested in the concerns of Mexican fruit pickers. He had a big heart for the underdog.

My father was never truly happy being a lawyer. One of the lessons that he learned from his career choice was the importance of doing what will make you happy, rather than what will make you rich. It is one of the important lessons that he taught me and what I try to pass on. Don't listen to anybody but your own heart, your own mind.

My father's social conscience was a significant part of his Judaism. His values influenced me. Before I was in politics I was the attorney for the Michigan Civil Rights Commission. I helped create a public defender's office for indigents, often unjustly accused of a crime. I believe that my father's sense of ethics has influenced my sponsorship of changes in the lobbying laws. I am proud of sponsoring The Whistle Blower Protection Act.

The creation of the State of Israel was an important issue for my family. I serve on the Senate Armed Services Committee and know something about liberation struggles and the rules of war. There is a difference between terrorism and violence. When Israel retaliates against a suicide bombing that kills young people in a pizzeria or a bat mitzvah, by going after a government target, that is an important distinction. You do not attack civilians. It's a difference between civilization and darkness. Civilians sometimes are killed when you are aiming at a military target, but you don't target civilians. If you do, you're violating international law. That's what the World Trade Center attack was about. It was an attack on civilians and on civilization. Our military response to go after Al Qaeda is a response to their attack. Our response is appropriate. That is the essential point to teach young people about this conflict.

My three daughters were born after my father died but I believe his values have been transmitted through our family. They are very proud to be Americans and very egalitarian. They dislike privilege and are very independent. They cherish making it on their own.

My wife and our three children, my brother and sister and their families continue to have Sunday dinners together. As a result, my kids and their cousins are very close. I think the greatest lesson I learned from my father was that a strong family is most important.

David Nadel is a veteran New York City policeman, currently working as a liason to the Jewish community. He was involved in the rescue events at the World Trade Center on September 11, 2001.

LT. DAVID NADEL

I get paid to make this city a safe place. As police liaison to the Jewish community I was involved with the events in Crown Heights in '91. I got a call from a local rabbi, "There's going to be trouble." I drove over. Things were heating up, but weren't yet out of control. Later that night, a small group of disorderly people started running through the streets. That's when the Chasidic man, Yankel Rosenbaum, was stabbed to death. Police made arrests at the scene. For the next few days there were sporadic incidents. On the third night large crowds were roaming the streets, setting stores on fire, throwing rocks and looting.

There were community leaders that I worked with from both the African-American and the Chasidic communities. A lot of people have worked very hard to make Crown Heights a nice place to live for everybody. It was just the one incident that sparked the unrest. The communities have worked well together since, with very few confrontations.

On 9/11 I was driving in Queens when the call came that planes had hit the World Trade Center. I put the siren on and joined a caravan of other emergency vehicles. I pulled into headquarters and moved toward the south tower with other police and firefighters. I heard this awful rumbling sound, looked up and saw the tower start to come down. I realized there was nothing I could do and that all those people in the building were going to die. I went numb. As it came down, a huge cloud of dust came tearing around the buildings. I felt my way along the fence next to City Hall, banged on the door, and an officer pulled me in. After the dust cleared, we were able to rescue and assist as many people as we could.

We helped people get to ambulances. I drove injured officers to area hospitals. We directed people to the Brooklyn Bridge. I helped to coordinate the delivery of heavy equipment at the rescue site. We coordinated escort patrols, since we had some of the only phones that were still working in Manhattan. A lot of what we did was to deliver personal items for the workers such as socks, underwear, boots, and helmets. It was all so overwhelming.

Afterwards, I was very fortunate to be part of a delegation that traveled to Israel to discuss terrorism with Israeli police. We shared not only experiences and information, but our feelings.

Raising my kids has been pretty typical. You go through little problems when they're little kids, medium problems when they're school kids, and as they get older, everything is a major issue. You get past it, and then everything's fine. One of my boys wears earrings and has his hair bleached and spiked. Who cares? That's what he's doing this week.

I want my kids to know that when you make a commitment you stand by it. I hope my legacy for them is that I did a very good job for a very long time. Once I decided to be a policeman, I decided to be the best policeman I could possibly be. ▪

Rabbi Morris Goldfarb, 90, was chaplain for Hillel at Cornell University from 1948 until 1980, and is currently Resident Scholar at Temple Emanu-El, Honolulu, Hawaii. He has two daughters, four grandchildren, and four great grandchildren. As a legacy to younger colleagues he states, "Try not to take yourself so seriously, try not to do everything, delegate, and leave a little to God.

RABBI MORRIS GOLDFARB

When my daughters walk into a room the place lights up. During their childhood I told them we observe traditional Judaism not because I am a rabbi but because this is what we do as a Jewish family. I told them never to feel obligated to do something because they were the daughters of a rabbi. Deborah loved to come with me to services to set up the wine cups. My oldest daughter was the first bat mitzvah in Ithaca, New York.

I believe that you can't change people by telling them what to do. At services I would ask, "What makes a Jew a Jew? What is of significance?" Kindness. Hospitality. These are Jewish values. The best teacher is what you do with your life.

I am now a resident scholar. People of all ages ask what Torah is about. There is a fad about Kaballah because we are in a society that wants instant gratification. People ask "What is Kaballah?" I say "spend ten years studying rabbinic literature, then we'll talk." You can't give an answer as if it is a pill.

My father was not learned but was a very observant man. He came from a shtetl near Cracow. Father was a congenial person, the mediator of the family. All squabbles came to him. He would always table-hop, a kibbitz here, a joke there.

We were seven boys and one girl, seven of us in one bedroom in the Bronx. There was a great deal of love between us. The older ones took care of the younger ones. My father moved us away from the East Side because my brothers were getting involved in Lepke Buchalter's Gang, a gang that ended up in the electric chair. My father, a tailor, managed to put bread on the table to feed eight children. On Shabbat we were together.

I was 15 when I graduated high school. I got a job for a sales distributor and brought home 4 dolllars a week. Then I applied to a program at the Jewish Theological Seminary Teachers Institute. I met my wife there. I went to a play in which my friend had the lead. He had a date that night. He said "Morris, will you take care of my date?" I did. I married her. She was the only woman I ever loved. At that time we learned about sexuality from our friends and ourselves, not our parents. We were naive and learned together, first with a little bit of necking. It was a different generation.

Fatherhood was wonderful. One day I was wheeling my baby daughter down the street. One of my congregants came to me later and said, "It's not appropriate for the Rabbi to do that." I was shattered, shocked. "What do you mean, not appropriate?" The rabbi had to be on a pedestal and couldn't do these ordinary things? I always felt I should be involved with my children. When they were babies I rolled around with them on the floor. I taught my daughters how to hold a bat and to throw a ball. I gave my children as much time as I could. I have been blessed a thousandfold by my children. ■

Frank London, composer and klezmer musician, is a founding member of The Klezmatics and Hasidic New Wave. Frank has played with LL Cool J, Yitzhak Perlman, Mel Torme, They Might Be Giants, John Zorn, Lester Bowie, and Chava Alberstein. He lives in New York City, with his wife, artist Tine Kindermann, and their two children, Louis and Anna.

FRANK LONDON

My kids are a gift, a blessing from a spiritual place. I see aspects of myself in them but they are totally their own selves. With a song I can describe the nuts and bolts of composition, but with children, their spirit, their souls, I don't know where their neshama comes from. This act of creation seems to come from someplace totally outside of us. My wife, Tine, and I are blessed to be the medium through which they entered the world.

Raising a kid is really a negotiation between being responsible for them and knowing when to give them space to make their own decisions. Often those two mandates can contradict each other. It's a fluid process and one of the hardest things about parenting. I had kids when I was 35, so I already had a life, I was an adult. Now, thank God, for the first time in seven years I haven't been changing diapers! Seven years of changing diapers! (No nostalgia for diapers.) When Tine and I are in the midst of all sorts of stress and everything's insane, I just look at her and say, "But these are the salad days! We're not in a nursing home and our kids are not getting arrested."

I am on the road touring so my time with the kids is erratic. Sometimes I am home a lot. They enjoy coming to KlezKamp and often travel overseas with me. Even though my schedule is difficult, it is not the big issue in our lives. I have a rather unique one. My wife is not Jewish. So, are our kids Jewish? I don't think they are. They need to be officially converted. I decided to talk to a few rabbis, to find out our options. Problem is you can find a rabbi who will give you any opinion that you want.

A Reform rabbi will say, "You're a Jewish father, raising your kids in a Jewish household, giving them a Jewish education, so—they're Jewish!" They don't need a mikveh and they can have Hebrew names. According to the Reform position, my son Louis would be "Loeb Simcha ben Ephraim" and Anna would be "Chana Batya bas Ephraim." The Orthodox say, "If Mom is not Jewish the kids are not Jewish. Throw them in a mikveh, then they're Jewish." Also, any convert is said to have been predestined to be a Jew and technically the child of Abraham and Sarah. So, if we have an Orthodox conversion Louis would be named "Loeb Simcha ben Avraham v' Sarah." My father, may he rest in peace, was named Avraham and my mother's Hebrew name is Sarah! So, if they do the conversion they get named after their Jewish grandparents. I met with a Reconstructionist rabbi who said, "Well, what do you believe? Is he Jewish because he is your son or because he converts?" This has to do with the essentialist pintele yid, there are very deep issues here. What do I truly believe?

When Louis was born it was an issue between Tine and I whether or not have a bris. I spoke with many people about it. Ultimately it is an issue of faith. There are no practical or pragmatic reasons for or against circumcision. We come into the world just fine, so why do anything? If you believe there is a deity that had made a specific command to do this, then it is an act of faith. It is done for spiritual reasons. So, we did it.

We had the bris in Berlin and it was an amazing comedy of errors. I know the head of the Jewish community who found us a mohel, the Jewish doctor on the army base. We were supposed to have the bris at the Juedische Gemeinde Haus, at the Jewish Community House, but the overly uptight security guard said that he had no orders to let anyone in. And of course it was raining. So, there we were in the rain, me, Tine, Louis, the mohel and about a dozen of our friends, including the head of the Jewish community. So, he says, "My office is about two blocks from here. Let's go." I was surprised how little Louis freaked out at the moment of circumcision.

Tine and I are now searching for a synagogue. We live in New York, in deep Jew world, and there are plenty of options but the kind of place I am looking for does not exist in our neighborhood. Egalitarian or non-sexist Chasidic. I want it all, the religiosity, spirituality, and ethnicity. I recorded an album in the hall of a local Lubavitcher synagogue. I'm very tight with the rabbi, For one year Louis went to the Hebrew school there. Ultimately the rabbi was way too right wing for me. On the other hand, Reform congregations are nice politically but they have terrible aesthetics. Surprisingly, I found this Conservative place in the neighborhood which comes closest to having it all.

My father was a very strong character. He loved to fish and had a perverse sense of humor. We reached a good point a few years before he died because I refused to discuss politics with him. He would say all sorts of racist, homophobic bullshit just to upset me, but I realized when he was around a real racist he would say the reverse to them. I think he just enjoyed annoying people. That's probably part of what I got from him.

At the time of his death, my brother and sister and I were talking about how we shared such strong but different aspects of him. Dad wanted to be a musician when he was young, but became a scientist instead. I have a photo of my father at work, bending over a bunch of test tubes. On the photo he wrote "Scientist at Work." That photo is on the cover of my dub Jewish record "Scientist at Work."

My father's best advice is a blessing and a curse. He taught me that since you have to work for a living, you should do something that you love. I think it's a great lesson and a very enlightened working-class attitude. He was totally supportive of my becoming a musician.

I went to the New England Conservatory of Music and studied world music, classical, jazz, rock and roll, salsa, Haitian music, African music, and Balkan music. At some point we were presented East European Jewish music by one of the teachers, Hankus Netsky. It was good, not the corny stuff I had heard growing up on Long Island at Jewish weddings. It became the source of a steady income. I had work every Saturday night and was getting paid well for it. Because I am Jewish, in the world's eye I am an authentic Klezmer player. Of course, non-Jews can play klezmer and I can play salsa or jazz.

Klezmer music has become a weird signifier of an imaginary cultural landscape, an association to the shtetl of Eastern Europe. It gives American Jews an ethnic identity within our multicultural society. In this way klezmer music has become important. Yet, I often wonder how much of our ethnic and cultural identity is an imaginary nostalgia. It doesn't really exist, but we assume it exists and as a result, it does exist.

I stopped doing Jewish weddings because the Chasidic wedding music became Americanized in a shlocky way.

I became involved with Chasidic and East European Jewish religious music. It is related to klezmer and that led to my project of composing niggunim, zmiros, chazzones, and integrating Jewish spirituality within my family life. That is when it all comes together for me, my professional and personal life. Singing niggunim, singing Shabbes table songs with my wife and children.

In the long run, I want my children to learn responsibility from me; to accept responsibility for themselves and for others. I want them to find a center in their lives but to understand how our actions effect others. That we can have a positive effect and be an influence for change. The idea has yiches.

Gene Bluestein, folk musician, professor emeritus of English and American Studies at California State Fresno, was author of many scholarly works, The Voice of the Folk, Anglish/Yinglish, *and* The Life and Death of a Polish Shtetl. *He established a Black Studies program and sponsored nationally known folk artists such as Pete Seeger to teach at the university. Gene and his children, Joel, Evo, Jemmy, and Frayda, have recorded CDs featuring Yiddish, English, Cajun, and world music. Dr. Bluestein died in 2002.*

GENE BLUESTEIN

My father was born in Besserabia and left in 1925 or 1926. He learned to cut furs from his father, and could make a coat with three skins less than anyone else. In the height of the Depression he had work, so we were not a poor family. We lived in Brighton Beach, a mixed neighborhood of Jewish, Italian, Irish, and black families. A black friend of mine used to call me "Coolstein".

My father was a son of a bitch, very self-centered, a bad husband, and a drunk. He liked to say, "I am the man nobody loves." He was mean to my mother whom I adored. He would run away until he got hungry. He always put pressure on me. He would say, "If you don't come with me, I won't leave you any money." I would say, "Who needs it?" So, I was on my own a lot.

There were no books in our family home, only newspapers. There was no Jewish learning from my father's side. The great cantor Moishe Oysher and his sister Fraydele, a Yiddish stage actress, were my first cousins though. We often heard Moishe perform in synagogues and on Second Avenue. Moishe and Fraydele used to sing as a gag a Yiddish song titled, "Ikh hob dikh tsufil lib tu zain oif dir in kas," which translates, "I love you much too much to have on you a hate." I was very much into jazz. There was a whole network of clubs in Brighton Beach running to Coney Island. I took drum lessons for 75 cents from a Broadway drummer named Sam Gershik. He used to say in a thick accent, "Play every note like a pearl." I played Dixieland with pickup bands in the local clubs.

One time I played hooky to see a Benny Goodman concert. The cops picked me up because I was underage. Next day my mother and I went to see the school principal. I showed up wearing a maroon shirt and solid green pants, a zoot suit. The principal said, "Look at him. He is a zoot suit killer." And my mother said, "I think he looks very nice." I had actually joined a gang. During high school we rented out a basement apartment, named it "Club Tempo" basically to shack up with girls, dance, and listen to music. To furnish it we sneaked into nearby apartments and took what we could, including the drapes. We climbed up fire escapes and went through people's homes like a buzz saw. My good friend made us a business card that said, "Club Tempo; It jumps and humps." However, when most of the other guys in the club bought guns, I quit the gang.

A friend's father got a job for me as a counselor at Camp Kinderland, a progressive Jewish children's camp in the Catskills. I had my first contact with Jewish intellectuals. Even the ten year olds had read Dostoevsky. I went on a wild reading binge and also became interested in folk music. Wonderful artists played at the camp: Pete Seeger, Woodie Guthrie, Paul Robeson. I taught myself to play guitar and banjo. I learned a repertoire of Yiddish and American music and also met my wife, Ellie.

In 1948 when Henry Wallace ran for president Ellie's father said, "If Wallace wins, I'll make you a wedding at Camp Kinderland." Wallace lost but we had the wedding anyway. I remember that Ellie and I were married by a drunk rabbi who tried to marry Ellie to her brother first. The rabbi gave me a chuppah pole to hold while he was handing her over to her brother! During the first few years of our marriage I was finishing my thesis and teaching. I went to the Appalachians to collect American ballads. You could shake a tree and five banjo players would fall out of it. I found wonderful stuff, both instrumental and vocal. I got a couple of grants and spent three years traipsing around in the backwoods.

I was so excited the first time that I became a father I got lost driving home from the hospital. My fatherhood has been a great joy. My oldest son, Joel, was a doll, never any problem. Evo was "Hamlet," he always had the blues and played a toy piano in his corner. Jemmy was an angel also, and Frayda was my doll. If I tried to discipline I would say, "Jemmy, if you do that I am going to spank you." Jemmy would reply, "If you spank me I will bite you!" I never hit any of them.

In our home we celebrated Judaism through music and song. We didn't take the kids to synagogue because I didn't like what was taught. My kids learned Yiddish and Jewish culture through Jewish folk music. The kids just gravitated to playing instruments and Frayda studied voice. Evo is one of the greatest autoharpists in the world.

While Joel was studying in Paris at the Sorbonne the entire family visited him. We received requests to play and began The Bluestein Family Band. We traveled the world playing in Japan, China, and Israel. In Israel we sang in Yiddish even though the audience would scream "sing in Hebrew!"

I have authored many articles about Yiddish. The use of Yiddish in English reflects the great American story of acculturation. Most people think of America as Anglo, English, Scottish, Irish, and that's it. No one ever dreamed the extent that minority cultures would influence all of American life. The word "chutzpah" is now a common word used in every American newspaper. The great achievement of minorities in America is so much has "crossed over." White kids wear their hats backwards and their pants low, and Yiddish words pepper the speeches of black politicians.

When the kids were young we celebrated Passover in music and song but there is no archeological evidence proving that the Exodus actually took place as we know it. There is no outside record of Moses, which is fine, because the story is a myth. After 2,000 years the myth is very strong. The idea of freedom is still very important and it is a great holiday, even though we don't know what really happened. I have to be really careful when I talk about this in our family because my granddaughter, Sarah, goes to a synagogue pre-school! ■

Theodore Bikel was born in Vienna Austria in 1924. After the Nazi annexation, his family fled to Palestine. After World War II he attended the Royal Academy of Dramatic Art in London, and began a distinguished career as an entertainer. He has appeared on Broadway, in hundreds of movies, television shows, operas, won an Emmy, an Academy Award nomination for his role in "The Defiant Ones," produced 16 albums of folk music, and has appeared over 2000 times as Tevye in "Fiddler on the Roof". He and his wife have two sons.

THEODORE BIKEL

My father's name was Joseph. My mother's name was Maria. Joseph and Mary. My name should have been Jesus! I was named after Theodore Herzl, the founder of modern Zionism. Herzl's picture hung over my bed all through my childhood.

My father was a very intellectual man who, because of the economic situation of the times, had to work at jobs that he didn't like. His university education had been interrupted by the First World War. After the war, he had to make a living, but spent his evenings reading, going to lectures. Ninety percent of all the people in the world do jobs they don't particularly like because they must feed their families. It's only the few fortunate ones, including myself, who have the luxury of making a living at what they love.

I wasn't raised religious. My father was a Socialist and a Zionist, but with a very strong sense of tradition. He could daven alongside the rest of them. In fact, ahead of the rest of them. High Holidays he would drag me from one shul to another. I became very well-versed in the religious ways, but I came from an intensely modern home that was a direct outcropping of the European Enlightenment. My sense of tradition is that you have to know the laws that you break.

The Nazis marched into Austria in March of 1938, when I was 13. Suddenly swastikas appeared everywhere. The Nazis came into my school. They beat us up. I remember that very well. There was a general assembly and the principal of the school said, "If in the first exuberance of joy over the reunification with our German brothers, excesses should happen, we will not be inclined to stop them." And the excesses did happen, of course.

I remember coming home bloodied after they beat me up at school. My father was very, very hurt by that. He cried. I hadn't seen him cry often.

My father was a veteran of Austrian Army in the First World War but that did not protect our family at all. We lingered for six months, trying frantically to get somewhere, anywhere. We took courses in Spanish in case we got visas to South America. The British gave out very few visas to go to Palestine, but father was able to get one. It covered my father, my mother, and me. It did not cover my grandmother, who stayed behind. We managed to get her out of Austria a month before the outbreak of the war. My father did something rather clever, because the Austrians had newly discovered their Nazi fervor. The border guards, of the Austrian-Italian border, were known to engage in chicanery, turning back people even though their papers were perfectly in order, paying no attention to proper formalities. So we took a long trip crossing all of Germany and France, went into Italy and took a boat from there to Palestine.

Theater had always had a pull on me. I did theater in school, a lot of plays, a lot of poetry. At first, being an idealist, I wanted to do something that the country needed. So I went to an agricultural school and a kibbutz, neglecting to observe that I had absolutely no talent or inclination for agriculture. I thought chickens were stupid animals. I stood on heaps of manure, singing songs about the beauty of the work that I wasn't doing.

The kibbutz, having taken note of the fact that I was very good at cultural activities, sent me to a seminar in Tel Aviv. There we were trained to put on plays, pageants, and festivals. We spent three intensive weeks learning from actors, from playwrights, from makeup men, all manner of things. I knew that that's where I wanted to be. So I went back to the kibbutz and regretfully bade them good-bye.

My father was afraid that acting was the most insecure profession that I could have chosen, and so he insisted, wisely, that I also pass the required university exams, in case I wanted to complete my education. Palestine was a British mandate at the time and I was admitted to the University of London. I was doing theater at the same time, which stood me in good stead as well, because it allowed me then to sit for exams at the Royal Academy of Dramatic Art.

I was in London when Palestine became Israel. In front of the Jewish Agency offices in Manchester Square there was jubilation, thousands of young Jews dancing and singing. It was a very heady day. Many of them went back, to be present at the formation of the state, most of them to fight. My colleagues who were in Palestine still, who were the same age as I, were impressed into service entertaining troops. They weren't doing fighting. My dilemma was, should I go back to Israel and entertain troops, or should I stay and perfect my craft, and render support from the outside as best I knew. I made the decision to stay. It was not an easy decision to make. My parents were back there and everything else. It turned out that I had contributed much more to Israel from abroad than I might have had I gone back.

I can't help being a Zionist, it's visceral. Anybody who grew up as I did, with extremely strong ties to the Jewish people can't walk away from it. You are a Zionist because you got it with your mother's milk. Or, better still, with your father's, whatever brew that is. But the complicated answer is, that this is not a simple world. History has changed and the position of the Jewish people has changed, and Israel has become a place of controversy. We are all part of that controversy, and have to take sides even within Israel. There are rifts and factions, and there are some destructive elements who would betray what I consider to be the raison d'être of the Jewish people's existence, which is a belief in all human dignity. There are struggles within Israel itself, within the Jewish people. The Jewish community in America tends to be very single-minded; anything that emanates from Jerusalem is okay with them, and that's not proper. Jerusalem is the seat of temporal, and therefore temporary, governments. And temporary governments can be right, can be wrong. They certainly mustn't be accepted blindly. Israel has 10, 12 major parties. People don't know how to deal with that, but one has to. I have quarrels with the ultra-Orthodox. I have quarrels with all fundamentalists; Jewish, Muslim, Christian.

My oldest son was born in '69 and the younger one in '71. I wasn't able to juggle a busy career at all. I was very often absent during phases of their development. Maybe my grandchildren, when they come, will have a better grandfather than my children had a father. I wanted to teach my sons a sense of morality. Not necessarily a morality rooted in a religious ethos, but that mere physical survival is not the only thing to be striven for. There has to be survival with values attached. You cannot survive while trampling on others' bodies, on others' souls, or on others' rights. I hope that I have transmitted these values as much by example as by just talking about them.

My oldest son was named after his maternal grandfather. His middle name, Simon, was named after my grandfather Shimon. My younger son was named after a maternal uncle. His middle name is Martin, after Martin Luther King, whom I knew from my activism in civil rights.

I am the president of the Associated Actors and Artists of America, part of the AFL-CIO, which includes the Screen Actors' Guild, and Actors Equity. I've always fought for the rights of working people. Actors have a passion; that permits those who employ them to exploit their passion. Actors would rather act than not act, and they would act for little money or no money at all. I think the dignity of labor demands that what one does should be recompensed properly. Since I have a voice and some modicum of eloquence, I figured I should put that voice to use to fight against the exploitation of all actors.

I have played Tevye in "Fiddler on the Roof" over 2000 times over 36 years. In my mind, Tevye was always my grandfather. My last tour with "Fiddler" was a year and a half, 463 and a half performances. The half performance was when

we were flooded out by a water main break during the first act. I never missed a performance. Eight shows a week.

I sang at my son's wedding. It was lovely! My son asked me to do it. I sang "Sunrise, Sunset," what else? For once it was about my family. About my son.

Bruce Maxwell of Studio City, California, is a successful businessman with two children, Yael and Sam.
He is a member of congregation Beth Chayim Chadashim.

BRUCE MAXWELL

We were raised in a Conservative home. My parents emphasized how important it was to respect Torah, the teachings of our people. The lesson I derived from Judaism was to have compassion towards others. It was a living Judaism in our house.

Growing up, there was no other way to have children other than to get married. I always knew I wanted to be a father. My grandfather was a person that would be on his knees to hug a child. I loved that. I wanted to be the kind of adult kids would look up to.

One of the toughest things was to come out to my parents. I remember growing up that to be a gay person wasn't proper. So I always hesitated to tell them, not knowing if they would be accepting. It took a lot of time before I had the confidence to talk to them. They had been very supportive through my divorce. Still, I wasn't sure. I told them there was something important I wanted to talk about. When I was finally able to speak, I spoke non-stop for 15 minutes. My mom said, "Is there anything that we can read so we can learn more?" One of the people that gave me the confidence to come out was their rabbi, Harold Shulweis. He gave a sermon at Rosh Hashana about accepting gay children.

There was never a specific time when I sat down with my kids and said, "I'm gay." They have just known that growing up. I decided I would raise my children to have an understanding that there are varieties of people in this world and to look beyond stereotypes.

Both kids still insist I tuck them into bed at night. They're good students, do their homework, but I still want to know that they're studying for a test. Several weeks ago, my 14-year-old daughter asked me at what age it would be appropriate for her to begin dating. I asked her the same question back. She had met a boy at Camp Ramah. Could they have dinner at a restaurant together? I thought that would be appropriate. She turned to me and said, "Thank you for being so understanding." My son is a big sports nut. I was assistant coach for their teams, which was fun. My dad was the coach of my Little League baseball team.

Most Friday nights, we light candles, sing the prayers, and have a family dinner. Beth Chayim Chadashim is the synagogue I came to when I first came out. It was the first gay/lesbian synagogue to be admitted to the Reform movement. It's a safe Jewish place that honors us as individuals. I've found a home for myself and for my kids.

My father gave me a High Holiday prayer book for my bar mitzvah. There was a dedication that he wrote. It was important to me then, and every time I read it, it's even more important.

"To Bruce, from your dad on the occasion of your bar mitzvah. Share it with your son as I did with you, and teach him to be a good Jew." I look at this now and can feel the moment that he gave it to me.

I try to guide my children towards success in their own lives. A successful person leaves behind people who look up to them, as I look up to my father. The idea of the honoring your parents is similar to honoring your children. I think as a parent, you honor your children. ■

Eric Rosenthal of Washington, D.C., is the founder of MDRI, an organization working for the international recognition and enforcement of the rights of people with mental disabilities. He is married to Lisa Newman, and has one daughter, Eliana Sophia. The interviews were done just before and just after Eliana's birth.

ERIC ROSENTHAL

Meeting Lisa made me decide to have a kid. I was being a workaholic, flying around the world, but then met Lisa and got married. I couldn't have imagined having kids before, but seeing Lisa with kids made it comfortable for me.

I'm very excited. I'm entering a total unknown. People say my life will change, and I have no idea what that really means. I have been so focused during Lisa's pregnancy, trying to get a report on Kosovo done. I've been frantically trying to get jobs finished so that I'll be freed up after the kid is born. I'm going to focus on my family, on my wife, on my child. I'm terrified. [laughing]

I had a wonderful childhood myself, and I felt that my parents did such a great job with me, that I could never do as good a job as they did. But being with Lisa, I feel more secure about that. I had a real friendship with my mother and father. I'd like to be my child's friend, too.

My father worked for U.S. government in foreign aid. Being Jewish meant wandering around the world and always being at home in my family. Wherever we went we found other Jews, even in some of the most remote villages of West Africa. We were in Upper Volta, and checked into a hotel in Bobo Dioulasso. The man behind the desk saw our name, "Rosenthal! You'll have to stay for our Passover Seder." He was a French Jew who ran the place. Even in parts of the world where there are very few Jews, the human rights activists are often Jewish.

This is also the first time in my life where I've really put down roots. It feels solid and comfortable. I'm hoping to live overseas for a few years in time. There's a line in our ketuba saying that our marriage is our home. Abraham's tent was open on four sides so that it would be always open to foreigners and strangers. We hope that our home will be a hospitable place too, where friends and relatives can come in. But a tent is a mobile thing, and wherever our tent may go, we'll carry Jewish culture with us.

I'm planning to be at the birth. I've gone to classes and held her hand during the amnio. The pregnancy has brought us much closer together. Lisa's been very dependent on me in some ways. She couldn't abide jello for a while, so I made her my grandmother's chicken soup. I'm learning that we can rely on each other, and I hope that positiveness will bring us together as we go through the intensive period of having a child.

We bought a house, a four-door car, a crib and more baby gizmos and contraptions than I had ever dreamed of. I'm not quite sure how they all work.

At the birth Lisa had a breech C-section. The one positive was that we knew when her birth was going to be. Lisa had no idea that the doctor had already started the operation. I was massaging Lisa's head, calming her down, and then the baby arrived incredibly quickly. I saw that it was a girl. They put

Eliana down, sucking out her mouth and cleaning her up. She screamed really loudly and then they handed her to me. The second they handed her to me she became quiet. She was unbelievably tiny. I positioned Eliana so that Lisa could touch her while being stitched up

She's two months old now, and often wakes up every hour. Nothing prepared me for this level of sleep deprivation. In the first few weeks I was walking around in a fog. I just didn't know how total a life change it was. When you have a baby, your life circulates around having a baby. It's been wonderful getting to know her, seeing every little facial expression and every little coo. She has been smiling in the last few days. It's a beautiful and wonderful experience. It makes it all worthwhile. Especially the coo.

I do diapering and feeding during the night. I usually take over around 11:00 or 12:00 midnight. There's generally a feeding between 2:00 and 3:00 in the morning and another feeding between 5:00 or 6:00 in the morning and then I hand her back to Lisa around 7:00. I sleep late and then I go to work, so Lisa does much more during the day than I do.

I founded a human rights organization that specializes in human rights for people with mental and developmental disabilities, both children and adults. A lot of my inspiration to do this work came from my father's example. The reason the organization was set up is that the established human rights organizations have had a blind spot for this issue. People with mental disabilities have human rights. Basic core protections against inhuman and degrading treatment and arbitrary detention are human rights. I have a grandmother who had manic-depression. It has flavored the way I view mental illness. I can't demonize mentally-ill people as being bad or evil, because I know my grandmother was a wonderful person. Traditionally there has been an avoidance of naming people after someone who was mentally ill. My grandmother had been a difficult person. Whenever we went up to Brooklyn to see her the screaming matches began the moment we entered the door, and I know that my mom had a hard time because of my grandmother's mental illness. Yet there was so much about her that permeated our family that was meaningful. I felt particularly close to her. She would be very creative. She would cook things that you would never dream of eating before. She came up with a patent for making furniture polish out of banana peels. The quality of passion, of experimenting, of loving life, is something that I got from my grandmother. And we named our daughter in part for her.

My father lives a few blocks away. He's making the transition into being a grandfather, and he comes over and both my mom and my dad help babysit. It's a wonderful thing to see him playing with her.

Mental Disability Rights International can be reached at www.mdri.org ▪

AL WONG

My parents did not have a religion per se but felt children needed to be associated with one. They were not Buddhists or Christians but sent me to a Catholic school. However, I was never baptized as Catholic. At times I had planned to do it, but it is rather fortuitous that it did not happen.

I forgot about religion until I met my wife Trudy. She is from a Conservative Jewish home so I studied Judaism. I took classes and was really embraced by Rabbi Nodel. I like Judaism as a religion because you have a faith and also learn to question, to analyze the Torah, the Talmud, and to interpret and reinterpret. In Judaism God is not to be feared. When you die your legacy is what you left behind.

After Trudy and I became engaged the rabbi said to me, "You know we need to convert you in a manner that her family will accept. I learned to daven and read Hebrew. I had the mikveh at the beach because there was not yet a mikvah in Honolulu.

I had been circumcised at birth but for my conversion went through the ritual again. The rabbi wanted everything to be kosher. A mohel came to my house to do a modified version. It involved the drawing of blood. (The things I did for my wife's family!)

When I told my parents that I was going to marry Trudy they said, "Two of the oldest cultures will be getting together here." We had an engagement ceremony where you pledge what you are bringing to the marriage. In old times it would be two goats. My father said the Chinese do something similar.

We keep kosher at home but in Hawaii it is hard to be totally kosher. When we used to eat at my parent's house we would have to bring kosher foods over. My father liked to make a big roast beef and he didn't understand our restrictions. We consulted with Trudy's father and he advised us to keep kosher at home but to honor my father in his home.

My son Ari is named "Ari Kol" which means "the lion's voice." My father-in-law, Aron, died six months before our daughter was born, so we named her Sharon. A friend from Israel explained that she should be called Shaaroni. Shaaroni has gone to Israel, Eastern Europe, and to China trying to find her roots. She is the one really interested in culture.

It is different being a father of a girl than a boy. When my son started driving, if he came home at midnight, no problem. At first I wouldn't let my daughter drive at night. Then when she was 18 I gave her a curfew. She felt that I had double standards. Shaaroni is my baby and woe be to anybody who'd hurt her. She prides herself that she has Daddy wrapped around her finger.

Our home is wide open to members of the Jewish community throughout the year—many come for Shabbat, Havdalah; the house is filled on the holidays. ■

Rabbi Schachter of Boulder, Colorado has held the World Wisdom Seat at Naropa University and is professor emeritus at Temple University. He is a central figure of the Jewish Renewal Movement, and founder of the Spiritual Eldering Institute. Born in Poland in 1924, he came to America in 1941. He has ten children: Miriam, Sholem Dov Baer, Yosef Yitzhaq, Akiva Eliyahu, Chana, Yonatan Gamliel, Alisa, Shalvi, Barya, and Yotam.

RABBI ZALMAN SCHACHTER-SHALOMI

My Papa Shlomo, olev hasholem, was a davener. Often he would take me to shul with him. One Rosh Hashanah, after he had finished the silent Amidah prayer, I saw that he had cried. I asked "Papa, why are you crying? "He said, "I'm crying because I talked to God." I asked him, "Does it hurt when you talk to God?" He replied, "No. I am crying because I let so much time go by since I talked to Him last."

Papa had a minhag that I have continued. He always bought his children very good tefillin. I do this and tell my grandchildren, "You're getting Cadillacs." I buy them really good tefillin, because I want them to be able to honor God. It places our action and our thinking at the disposal of God's will.

When my first child, Mimi, was born I came to New York and met my old teacher, Reb Shmuel Lavitan, an aged Chabad chasid, who taught us on the higher level. He asked me, "What are you learning from your daughter?" It was a wonderful question to ask, because I didn't consider such a thing, to look at a newborn and say that I had to learn from the child. That trained me in watching children.

I think it is important for fathers to participate in all stages of a child's birth and welcome into the world. I think it is significant for the father to make the first cut on the umbilical cord. For a father to do that means to take on responsibility. There is a continuity from father to grandfather all the way to Abraham, and that's a very powerful thing.

The Earth is a living being. Every species is part of the vital organs of the planet. Religions are part of the vital organs of the planet. No religion can claim that it is the sole carrier of the life of the planet. Jewish mitzvahs have to do with staying in harmony with the cycles of life. Pesach is at the full moon of the vernal equinox and Sukkot happens at the full moon of the autumnal equinox, they're plugged into life.

There are are no models today on how to become older. You no longer have grandparents living in the same household with grandchildren That is what brought me to the spiritual eldering work. When children see that the parents of that older generation, instead of being crabby, are still holding a kind of spiritual center in themselves, then they can honor that. I teach people how to own their lifelong experience and to become mentors, wisdom-keepers for the younger generations, to pass on the legacy. ■

Sandy Levine, M.B.D., owns and operates the Carnegie Delicatessen in Manhattan.

SANDY LEVINE

The restaurant started in 1937. I married the owner's daughter, so I became an "M.B.D." (Married the Boss's Daughter). I started on the top and worked my way down.

My father had a candy store. Malteds, egg cream, cigars, comic books, and candies. We lived above the store, and my father opened up at 5:00 in the morning. He instilled in us a work ethic. I used to work for a quarter an hour. Pizza was 15 cents, a coke was 10 cents. So you had lunch for 25 cents, and if you worked another two hours, you had 50 cents, you went to the movies. For a dollar, you had a terrific day. Another thing he always taught me was "Remember the bottom." A dishwasher is just as important as a cook. Without clean dishes you can't serve your food. We have people that have been here 44 years. We try to take care of all our employees. My father-in-law always said, "The buck stops here." He grew up on Truman and Roosevelt.

I attribute the success of this restaurant to being hands-on. We make our own food. We were one of the first to give the gargantuan sandwiches, where you can't put your mouth around it. Even if the sandwich was $1.95 and your customer leaves hungry, he forgets that he paid only $1.95, but remembers that he was hungry. So we give a lot of portions.

It's an ethnic Jewish deli that attracts all races, creeds, and nationalities. We have eggs. We have cheese. We have the corned beef, the tongue, the brisket, Matzo balls, chicken in the pot, flanken in the pot, and the chopped liver.

Most of the stars don't live here any more. But, when they're in New York, this is a "must stop". They come back to get the thrill of a good matzo ball soup, a good frankfurter, a good corned beef. Everywhere else it's an imitation.

President Clinton comes in here, a good 'ol boy. We gave him a "Broadway Danny Rose", which is named after Woody Allen, who shot a movie here. That sandwich is about a pound and a half of meat. He had a slice of cheesecake, too.

During Desert Storm in '92, Bob Simon of CBS was held captive. When he was released, he went to London. They asked him "What can we do for you?" He says he wanted a pastrami and corned beef sandwich from the Carnegie Deli. So, CBS called us up and said they need a corned beef and pastrami "for travel." They sent it on the Concorde. We made every newspaper in the world!

Mel Brooks is the conventional type of Jewish person. The chopped liver, corned beef and pastrami. Jerry Lewis comes in, and all he wants is knockwurst and beans! Larry King comes in, also franks and beans. Somebody's on location, we ship them a sandwich. They're a little crazy. For $30.00, they have a corned beef sandwich, but this is America, and God bless America.

My favorite thing to eat in the Carnegie Deli is the cheese blintzes. Everybody comes in for corned beef and pastrami. But cheese blintzes, the best! People come in and ask for our recipes, but we guard them just like Coca Cola.

When my kids were growing up I would tell them to work hard. Don't be lazy. Stay in school. Have a good work ethic. They all were bat-mitzvahed, but I didn't cater it. Let someone else do the work! ■

Dr. Lichtman of Richmond, Virginia is a divorced father of two children, who shares joint custody. He is an associate professor of pharmacology in the School of Medicine at Virginia Commonwealth University.

My wife reverted back to Christianity after our divorce. So my children's Jewish education and identity is pretty much on me. Since we have different religions I teach them that there is one God, and that we have different ways of observing. I want my children to have a strong sense of identity and Judaism plays a role in that. There is a strong continuity from generation to generation.

As "Mr. Mom" every other week, I lead a schizophrenic existence but I am getting into a groove. My kids go to Rudlin Torah Academy. The standards are high and the kids enjoy themselves. We do Shabbes dinner at home and on Saturday we hang out. The kids will sleep in a bit in the morning but we do go to services.

I remember walking to shul with my father. He'd carry his tallis bag. We had to walk through a bad neighborhood, and there was anti-Semitism. My father walked very proudly. I'd cringe and wish, "Can we take off our yarmulkes? Let's just drive." I learned from my father's example. He stood fast; committed and resolved. He was very devoted to all of us. Unfortunately, my mother got ill when I was in high school and she became the focal point of my father's life.

My mother had breast cancer which metastasized into a brain tumor. She lived for seven more years. My father spent his time taking care of her. His commitment to my mother affected me. I learned a tremendous sense of loyalty and self-sacrifice.

When my daughter Elaine was born, my sister asked, "What do you want her to be when she grows up?!" I said, "Anything she wants." I just want her to be happy and love what she does. I'd like that for each of my children. Yet, it is hard being a single father.

I've taken JCC parenting classes. We talk about children's behaviors and discuss strategies. It is good to express empathy to your children while disciplining them, and not to rub their face in it. I don't spank my kids. Hitting a child only teaches them to not do a behavior while the parent is around. It does not really teach them to internalize right from wrong.

My daughter is highly verbal and difficult to argue with. Often, I need to realize, "Hey! I'm the parent…" My son is more physical. At one point, I would lose any kind of power struggle, no matter what the punishment. I might say, "No TV for the week." He would say, "Fine, why not for the month?" I've learned to wait and talk to him when he is calm.

One time I couldn't get a babysitter so the kids had to come to one of my evening lectures. I got them snacks and games and sat them in the control room off of the lecture hall. Within two minutes, Patrick is out of the control room. I'm lecturing, cardiovascular pharmacology. I look up, and he's raising his hand as though he's asking a question, then suddenly starts walking down the aisle. The students start laughing. I'm thinking to myself, "Oh no, he's going to be defiant in front of my class!" I said, "Excuse me. Turn around and you go back, and I'll be done in an hour." As he was walking away, I said, "Well, someone's not going to be getting ice cream." And then my students started yelling, "But he has an ice cream!"

Parenting…it's always a work in progress. ■

Sanford Schulman of Detroit Michigan is a criminal defense attorney, married with two children. When his best friend died, Sanford became an active 'godfather' to his friend's two-year-old son.

SANFORD SCHULMAN

I remember very clearly the first night that my newborn daughter came home from the hospital. I couldn't sleep. I was worried, whether she cried or not. So, for awhile I slept with her on my chest. I thought about family and felt that here was a brand new part of me. At that moment I realized I would do anything to protect her, like jump in front of a train without blinking an eye, or lay on a grenade. There is no question about it.

And so when my best friend, Joe, died of cancer, there was no question about that either, I would be there for his son, Alec.

I was married in August of 1992 after Joe was already very ill with stomach cancer. He hung in there for my wedding and gave the greatest speech. Death was all over him. There we were standing under the chuppah and he's putting on my kitl. And the kitl is what you wear at a wedding and at a funeral. A month later I am dropping off a kitl at his funeral.

According to *Pirke Avot,* (the Ethics of our Fathers), the greatest gift that you can give a friend is to help guard his family and possessions as your own. Joe and I never exactly spoke about my being there for Alec. We didn't really need to. We were like branches from the same tree. Joe just knew I would do what ever was necessary for Alec.

After Joe died, I was able to spend quality time with Alec because my wife and I did not have children right away. Once we did, Alec knew that he was always welcome in our home but that he also needed to carve out a life with his mother, their friends and relatives. So, my relationship with Alec is not exactly well defined. I am not a blood relative. His mother will eventually find someone. I am not a replacement father. I am a male role model. I am basically the guy he talks to and hangs out with. I help Alec with his Jewish studies. We also like to act goofy and just have fun. I didn't think it my role to ever really discipline him. At special times Alec just likes to sit with me and hear stories about what his father was like.

I met Joe when I was 13 or 14 through a Bnai Brith chapter. We both went to college in Michigan. Being with Joe was always like getting three flavors in one scoop of ice cream. He and I believed in having what we called "self-inflicted fun". Joe performed in theater and was unquestionably the funniest guy around. He could make your soul laugh. He did his own version of Michael Jackson's moonwalk, even when we were touring in England at Buckingham Palace. He would play Ultimate Frisbee on rainy days, and just nose-dive into mud puddles. We used to rent cars and go on these long trips. We would listen to a tape, like Steely Dan, over and over again for hours. We paid attention to everything in life. Joe and I shared this attitude that it is not the destination but the journey that is most important. Time is precious.

Sometimes while praying, while davening, I feel so lucky that I have it all—wife, children, healthy parents, a good job. I remember in yeshiva, questioning the teacher. I liked to push the envelope and once asked, "Rabbi, what if none of it is true? What if you learned that there is no God and no Torah?" He looked at me and answered, "It would not matter. I have a wife and beautiful family that are dedicated to me, a community that supports me, and a day off to be with all of them." And this is the lesson that my father taught me, the importance of family.

My father is a quiet, almost introverted, well-organized man, who did it all for his family. He is not the life of the party, the guy with the cigar hanging out of his mouth, dealing cards in Vegas. He was never a schmoozer. My father was a schoolteacher. He put his money in the bank, and spent his Sundays at home. I think of him as defending me like you would the pupil of your eye. The family was his main vision of a good life. Yet, with me he is argumentative. In that respect he helped me appreciate the field of law. Now I joke with him and say, "Dad, if you don't put a hundred and fifty bucks down on the table, you don't get an hour of my argument."

I now work half of the day out of my home so I can be with my kids during the afternoon. My daughter understands that I am a criminal defense attorney, but she doesn't always get exactly what that means. During Yom Kippur my daughter was asked in her school what she was sorry for, for teshuva. She stood up and said, "I am sorry that my daddy's best friend is in prison." Of course, I had to explain to her that it was my client that was in prison. She understands that I go before a judge and try to help people tell both sides of a very sad story.

Right now my daughter is in that four-year-old stage where she thinks that I am the "bravest, strongest, fastest, and most smartest man…in the world!" I would love to keep it that way for a very long time. ▪

Rabbi Shmuel Simenowitz, his wife Rivki, and their children Tova and Shlomo, live on Sweet Whisper Farms, in Readsboro, Vermont. It is Vermont's only shomer-shabbos, kosher, organic, horse-powered maple sugar farm. Rabbi Simenowitz is a former entertainment lawyer, musician, and stand-up comedian.

RABBI SHMUEL SIMENOWITZ

I was brought up in a Conservative home on Long Island, attending yeshivas. I was a problem child. I was funny and intelligent and gifted and bored and challenged, all in the same day. I feel like I was raised religious but then at one point, I fell off the wagon. I became completely engrossed by popular culture. I had to claw my way back. As an entertainment lawyer I was making tons of money and hanging out with rock stars, but I did not own my life. I had big houses, big cars, and very bad values. You know, you think your company works for you but you become a slave to it. So, I became very unsatisfied and started to search for an alternative lifestyle. If you have a tree and it's bent over, you want to make it upright. I started moving towards religion. I started clawing my way back, started keeping kosher again. My first experiences with religious wisdom were intellectual. I devoured learning. I didn't read a book, I ripped the heart out of it. I had a thirst for knowledge of everything. I still do.

I've come full circle. I was raised by a father who loved horses. His father loved horses. So, I began thinking of how to combine my love of the land, animals, and agriculture with my marketing and business savy. The first step was to move away from New York to Vermont. And then things just evolved. I read Torah every week. My family became kosher. We bought the horses, the chickens. We had to find appropriate places to school the children. And eventually I joined Chabbad. I used to

joke that I converted but now I say I have "upgraded."

Jewish parenting is, in a sense, making a better world by putting out your message through your kids. Your kids cause you to be a better person and to examine things. And I want my kids to have the best of all worlds. By the time Tova was nine years old she was driving a team of draft horses and learning Talmud. Recently we went to a conference on Jews in rural areas. And my kids realize that they're the role models. If you ask my six-year-old son what his favorite thing to do is he'll say, "Walking to synagogue holding my father's hand." So, I have from my children "Naches Incorporated." They seldom, if ever watch television. My kids have pen pals. They write plays. They put on shows. Before Rosh Hashana my kids and I teach others about bees and how honey is made. They are completely involved with taking care of our farm.

I teach my children and others that the laws of Torah are thousands of years old and that they command us to act as stewards, not masters of the earth. Unfortunately, today if you can't master something in ten seconds or less it's not worth having. And what you really see in a Jewish agrarian setting, and what I teach is process. You know, where does maple syrup come from? It doesn't come from a jar. Somebody went out, cut a trail, tapped a tree, hung a bucket, and collected sap. And all things are connected, the seasons, the harvest, the holidays, how we treat the animals and use the land. So, I use the process of making maple syrup as a metaphor for teaching Torah. My farm is both kosher and organic. I produce a kosher maple syrup. In the sugar shack, when the tree sap boils it foams up. Traditionally the way most folks stop this is with a fat based substance. The old-timers would take a piece of pork fat and suspend it on a string right at the point where the foam would hit. Then the foam would subside. People "in the know" are uncomfortable that their syrup is processed with pork fat. What I use is extra-virgin olive oil. It is both organic and kosher.

I am now involved with this "eco-shtetl farm" project with this Chabadnick in Amherst. This means I need to become an expert on Shabbos. There are intricate laws about working the land and caring for animals. We need rest and so do the animals. We can't carry the animal food outside to them unless we have an eruv. A dog cannot wear its collar with the tags on it because that is a form of carrying but a horse can wear a halter. We can't collect the eggs on Shabbos. So, all of these laws really come alive for us. We don't turn on the lights. We don't use electricity. We don't use the phone. We don't drive. We don't cook. Shabbos is a wonderful time here. We wear farm clothes all week long but not on Shabbos. Everyone is dressed to the nines. The house is clean, there is a big meal, lots of singing, and it is really beautiful.

We bring farm programs to the schools, tied in to the Jewish holidays. Before Rosh Hashana, we'll bring down bees, show how honey is made. We'll bring down chickens and show where eggs come from. At Tu B'shvat, we'll show them about sugaring. We've had Jewish Youth at Risk programs come up here and spend Shabbos on the weekend. We davened and learned and sang. They just really needed someone to listen to them and pay attention. I took each kid out for a wagon ride, just one-on-one. We got to talk. Everyone was almost in tears when they left.

We just finished Succos last week. Succos in Vermont! The foliage is beautiful. The whole world was our succah. We always make our succah out of recycled materials. Old shutters, barn doors. One year we were in the succah, my wife and I, sipping tea and singing late. And we heard rustling. And sure enough, there were coyotes coming down. We resolved it very pragmatically. We said, "It's time to go inside!" ▪

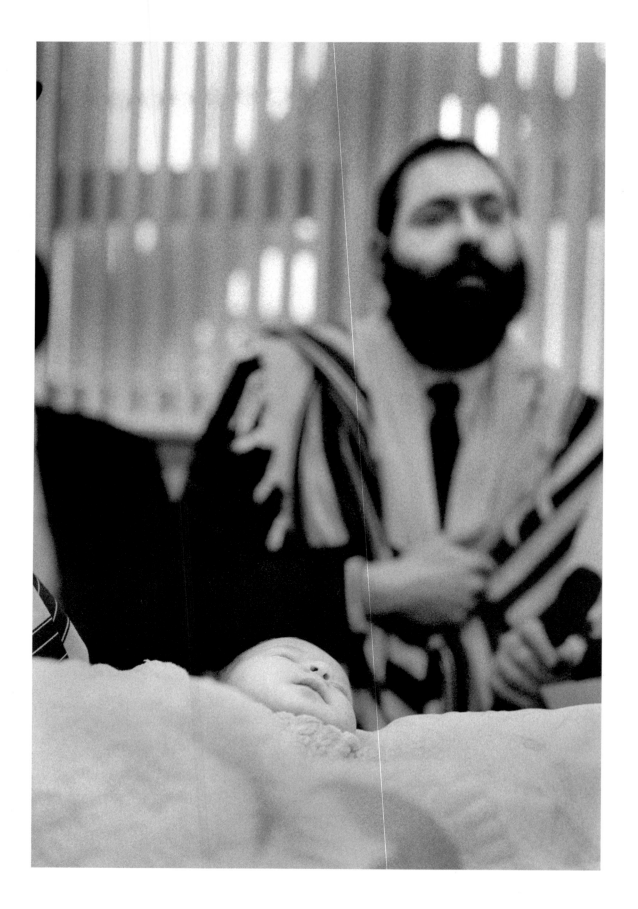

Rabbi Yosef Yitzchak Jacobson of Brooklyn teaches Jewish law and kabbalah at the Rabbinical College Chovevei Torah and is a noted lecturer and writer on Judaism, mysticism, and psychology.

RABBI YOSEF YITZCHAK JACOBSON

I grew up in Crown Heights, Brooklyn at the feet of the Lubavitcher Rebbe, Rebbe Menachem Mendel Shneerson, a great spiritual master, a genius in presenting Judaism in a very relevant and stimulating way. As I grew up, I began to encounter people who felt that Judaism was obsolete and had no relevance to their modern and progressive lives. I felt compelled to start sharing the wisdom I was fortunate to learn from my master. I began speaking and writing. Now, I travel internationally to lecture about Judaism, its contemporary applications and its timeless perspectives on timely events.

My father was born in 1933 in Moscow. His father was Simon Yakobashvili, a Georgian Jew. My grandfather was part of an underground operation founded by the previous Lubavitcher Rebbe, the late Rabbi Joseph Isaac Shneerson to preserve Judaism under Stalin. The communists attempted to eradicate every vestige of Judaism and the Rebbe created the underground to keep synagogues, mikvahs, and schools open. When my father was five, the KGB took his father away. It was Shabbes, Friday night, and my grandfather was in the middle of making kiddush over the wine. They sentenced him to death but changed the verdict to 25 years in Siberia.

My father did not see his father for years. Through bribery and diplomacy, my grandfather was liberated near the end of the war. My father grew up in a painful and tragic era, but has also been a witness of extraordinary heroism. I think this twofold element has characterized his life. He made a career out of journalism. He opened up his own Yiddish weekly, the

Algemeiner Journal, which he still edits and publishes. My father is very courageous, a real fighter for Jewish causes. What I learned from him was the inspiration to stand up to the world when there is a situation that is threatening Jewish survival and Jewish life. My father taught us by example not to remain silent when injustice rears its ugly head.

The greatest gift in the world is the opportunity to create another generation of children, who will carry on the torch of Jewish history and identity. This is embedded in the blood and sinews of a Jewish father. Nothing is as powerful, as potent, or important as creating healthy children: physically, psychologically, and spiritually. We are all mortal. Our brains are limited. Our hearts are limited. Even our dreams are limited. There's only one activity, through which we become infinite. And that is when we invest our energy in our children.

The first story that we learn about a Jewish father is the story of Abraham and the sacrifice of Isaac. My approach is based on Chasidic teachings. God did not want Abraham to kill Isaac. God wanted Abraham and Isaac to experience a totally different type of love for each other. All human love, as powerful as it is, has parameters. We remain defined within our own biological nature and we love our children from that space. What the binding of Isaac accomplished for Abraham was, God said, "Give me your child." A natural father would say, "It's mine! It belongs to me!" But God says, "It is a gift that I gave you. I want my gift back." Abraham rose to the occasion, the most difficult challenge in the world, and was ready to give his son back to his Creator. The moment he was ready to give up ownership over his son, God turned to him and said, "I do not need him. You take him back." When Abraham returns with Isaac, they love each other in an absolutely new way, in an infinite and eternal way. It is no more about "I love you because it feels good and it is natural." Now it has become, "I love you beyond my nature. I love you with a super-human love."

Even our most beautiful and noble qualities are defined by the limitations and restrictions of our own nature. Even the love of parents to children has limitations. Sometimes parents are capable of doing unloving things, consciously or unconsciously. Fathers love their children, but sometimes if their child ruins something on their computer all hell breaks loose. Don't you love your child more than your computer? The answer at that moment is no. The story of Abraham and Isaac was trying to change that forever. It became the legacy of Jewish fathers. God tells us, "I want you to be able to love your child with divine love, with infinite love; I want that your love

to your child should not be bound by your mortal and human nature; I want the love to transcend the limits of the human condition, to go above and beyond all calculations." God wants us to love our children in the same way He loves us. But as long as we are not ready to give up the finite relationship, we can't acquire the infinite relationship.

My children are very young. When they wake up very early in the morning, it is my domain. I play with them, change the diapers, give them cereal and milk, and just hang out with them. My second job is in the evening when I come home from work. I help bathe them, put on their pajamas, change the diapers, and get them to bed. I sit in their bedroom, we sing songs, we schmooze. We sing a lot of songs that my mother used to sing with me when I was a child. Yiddish songs like "Afen Pripachik": "On the fire stove burns a little flame, and the home is warm, and the rebbe with the little children are learning Alef Bes." We sing Hebrew melodies, Chasidic melodies. Then we do the Shma together and we pray together

for peace in Israel and in the world. It is a tremendous time of bonding, one of the highlights of my day. At that moment I can't thank God enough for the gift to see my children growing up.

I want my children to enjoy happy and fulfilled lives. I hope that they develop the confidence to maximize their potentials, to blossom and live life to the fullest. I would like to see them continue the heroic choice of our forefathers: to be obsessed with good, and horrified by evil. I pray that they make the world a better place than it was when they entered it; bringing it one step closer to redemption. ■

Michael Turniansky is a computer programmer from Baltimore, Maryland who works out of his house and homeschools his four sons: Baruch Noah, Rashi, Yisroel Hillel, and Yehuda Chaim Mendel.

MICHAEL TURNIANSKY

According to Talmud a Jewish father has four duties to his sons. His priority first is to teach them Torah, then to teach them a trade, how to swim (which is meant literally and how to survive in the world), and to find them a wife. That part I am not so worried about yet.

We practice our Judaism everyday. When they wake up in the morning we say the prayer thanking God for restoring our soul and for blessing us. Getting all of them up, dressed, and eating breakfast can be quite a challenge. On Monday mornings we do the week's Torah reading. I have a book called *My First Parsha Reader*. My little one will color the pictures. My six year old likes to read to his little brother. My four year old is working with recognition of Hebrew letters. We use the computer for our lessons. My wife found a screen saver that displays pictures of Israel. My oldest son just devours books. He read the fourth Harry Potter book in two days. He self-censors books that are non-Jewish and deal with Christmas. I have read the Potter books and have no problem with them. In my day, I was an epic Oz fan.

My children understand the difference between what is Jewish and what is not. They know that I want them to respect their fellow human beings and to be comfortable with their own Jewishness. I want them to understand that the laws of Judaism are important. They are not envious of the majority culture and don't feel any kind of loss. Since they don't go to a public school they're not bombarded by images of Christmas.

On the other hand we will drive down the streets in December and say, "Gee that is a nice display of lights."

We haven't discussed the Holocaust in depth yet because I do not want to frighten the younger ones. They know that the Hanukkah, Purim, and Passover stories are about persecution. For Passover I teach them that every Jew is supposed to see himself as if he has gone out of Egypt. I tell them that if God had not taken us out of Egypt we might still be there today. I teach them that when Maschiach comes it will all be straightened out.

Right now, they are active, energetic boys. My discipline depends on the particular level of offense. I respect the fact that they have lots of energy but there is punishment in the form of time-out for pushing, shoving, and hitting. There can be removal of privileges such as watching TV or playing on the computer. Except for the little one they all share a room. So, there is a lot of activity at bedtime. I try to nip it in the bud. Like all parents I work on controlling my temper. Counting to ten often helps.

My father, Simon, stressed the value of education. He regretted that he did not get a college education, so he wanted that for us. Yet, even without a college degree he became an electronic engineer and built satellites for a living. He has a very strong work ethic. He built everything in the house, the kitchen, bathroom, living room. He did all the installations, wiring, and plumbing. To this day I still call him with my problems. ▪

Joseph Menashe, of Portland, Oregon, is descended from Sephardic Jews from Rhodes, Greece. A former rock and roll keyboardist, he runs a successful real estate business. He has two children, Aaron and Andrea.

JOSEPH MENASHE

My father came from the island of Rhodes. The family lineage goes back to Izmir, Turkey. The Sephardic lifestyle, foods, and rituals were handed down to me. My Jewishness was the Sephardic Jewishness, different from my Ashkenazi friends. My mother is one of the best bakers of Sephardic goodies. Spinach boyos, ponderikas, parmakies, wonderful foods. In synagogue it was primarily Hebrew and Ladino. The Sephardic melodies are different, much more melancholy.

Ever since my wife converted, I'm learning more about Judaism. I went to all of the conversion classes with her, and became sort of a born-again Jew. I'm trying to create a more active Jewish lifestyle for my kids. We celebrate Shabbat. They're with me part of the time, they're with their mother part of the time, who's not Jewish. So their Jewishness all comes from this house. Originally I tried to bring them up exposing them to both religions, their mother's and mine. Finally, through the support of Joanne, I got to the point where I said, "Wait, that doesn't work. They have to know who they are." So, I involved them in religious school. My daughter studied Hebrew and had her bat mitzvah, and my son was confirmed. I wanted my children to have more spirituality than I saw them having, I saw that there was a void in their lives. Even though I was brought up Jewish, I didn't embrace it, it was just kind of there. And I wanted them to feel, not only that they are Jewish, but to feel that they were part of being Jewish.

I went through an identity crisis when I was in my 20s, in 1973 before the Yom Kippur War. I graduated from college and travelled around Europe and Israel. I was having conflicts with my Jewish identity. I didn't know where I was with it. I stopped in Rhodes, Greece, where I visited the old synagogue which my grandmother used to talk about. On the front is a plaque listing the Jews that were murdered. The names were recognizable as families I've known from the Sephardic synagogue in Portland. Then to see my own family name up on the plaque. That drives the reality home real quick. Then I went to Israel, and in Jerusalem I wanted to buy myself a star or a Chai. I got a Chai because it represents life. It was a very spiritual decision for me. I wore it around my neck ever since, and never took it off until my son became 13, when I gave it to him. It was my way of passing on my spirituality to him. Now he wears it and never takes it off.

Now that Aaron has finished his confirmation, his class will be going to Israel, and he's excited about that. So I feel that I'm doing my part as a Jewish parent now. I'm starting to fulfill my responsibilities.

I want kids to be happy, to have a good life, to do good deeds, to treat people with kindness. To honor me and my family by how they conduct themselves. Aaron was involved in a mitzvah project at a home for abused children. They brought art supplies and played basketball with the kids. Andrea is an animal lover, so she's donated time at the Humane Society. They're going to be out of the nest before you know it, and those values really seem important.

Yaacov Hammer is a private consultant, photographer, and trainer in Washington, D.C. He met his wife, Resna in the Peace Corps. They have two daughters, Rachael and Tamar.

YAACOV HAMMER

There are more explicit religious texts prescribing women's role in the family than there are for men. Torah commands us to observe the mitzvahs, and that we are obligated to provide for our children's education, job training, and to find them a marriage partner.

I daven every day. The act of binding tefillin creates a profound sense of intimacy with God, that one is not the center of the universe.

My father was a man of integrity, a jeweler who came from the generation that kept their word. My parents were very much in love. They had a partnership and this formed my ideal of marriage.

I am of the generation that thought President Kennedy was addressing important issues. I joined Peace Corps and was sent to the Dominican Republic. There I met my wife, Resna. She was also a volunteer, the only female American around. We started talking, became friends, and married three years later.

At first my parents were not pleased with my marriage, because Resna is West Indian. They did not speak to me for a couple of months, but fortunately consulted with a relative. He said, "You have a choice. You can have your son or you can lose him." So, my parents called. After they visited, my mother called my wife every Sunday for as long as she lived. Resna became like a daughter to my parents.

I never really think about my family as "multicultural." I was asked, "what is it like having an interracial marriage?" and I said, "I really don't know because I don't have anything to compare it with. It just seems normal." I have not experienced racism within the Jewish community towards my family. My wife was the treasurer of our synagogue, and is now the president of the sisterhood.

While developing community projects in New York I frequently went to services in Crown Heights and invited to meet the Lubavaticher Rebbe. My impression was that the Rebbe was just the space of integrity. His actions, thoughts, and words were all the same.

One night I was housed in an Orthodox home and heard the mother say to her daughter, "When you are 18 you will be old enough to wear lipstick." I thought, "This conversation is no different than in my home." As we became observant I was clear to my girls that men and women are equal. I explain that Orthodox practices make distinctions, but it does not mean men are better than women.

The most important Jewish value I taught them is tikkun olam. We have a responsibility to be of service. I am very proud of Rachael, who started a sorority at Columbia University, because there was no place for observant Jewish girls.

Our family has grown. I became a grandfather. I was the person who held the baby during the bris. And they named the baby for my father. ◾

Gerson Panitch, father of three, is a lawyer in private practice, on the board of directors of D.C.-based Gifts for the Homeless, Inc., and is a member of the board of Beth Sholom Congregation and Talmud Torah in Potomac, Maryland, were he serves as liaison to the Social Action Committee. Every year on Christmas day, Gerson leaves his modern Orthodox neighborhood dressed as Santa Claus, and delivers gifts to children in Washington, D.C.-area homeless shelters.

GERSON PANITCH

I have not yet had to explain to my young children why I dress up as Santa Claus. But when the time comes, the answer will be simple. It is a mitzvah to help people in need. Like my father and mother, who taught me the meaning of tikkun olam through their own actions, I am doing a mitzvah by brightening the lives of some of the neediest people in our community. The December 25th program, organized through the D.C. JCC, gives me, and hundreds of other Jewish volunteers who participate by cooking meals, distributing clothing, painting shelters, or visiting the sick, an opportunity to perform a double mitzvah. We not only help the homeless, but we relieve non-Jewish social service workers so that they may enjoy their holiday with their families.

It is only one thing that I do, among what is usually a very traditional Jewish life. I've received phone calls from local area Hebrew School teachers who ask me to come in costume to their classes and speak about my reasons for doing this. Its one thing to go to an inner-city homeless shelter dressed as Santa, but I'm just not comfortable walking into to a Jewish institution dressed that way. Judaism is filled with its own beautiful symbols and traditions that bind us together. I want to be careful not to confuse children into thinking that it is appropriate to dilute our heritage with the traditions and symbols of another religion. So the Jewish Santa stays in the depressed neighborhoods of downtown Washington.

Of course, when I walk into a homeless shelter dressed as Santa and encounter other Jewish volunteers serving meals or entertaining the homeless children, I can't help but shout "Good Yontev!" Folks tend to look a bit confused.

I have always felt a sense of reverence for my father, a rabbi for many years at Congregation Beth Israel, a traditional Conservative synagogue in Milwaukee. In our family home we lived and breathed Judaism. My father officiated at my bar mitzvah and at my wedding. I remember being the age that my son is right now, which is about four years old. My father used to bring me into synagogue and seat me in the front row. He taught me that I have to be very respectful during services. Being an "R.K." (rabbi's kid) meant that I had to learn early on how to avoid doing anything that might be viewed as an embarrassment. When I wanted to be out of the limelight, I had to sort of play the shadows.

There are some fathers who will let their children do whatever they want, but not my father. In my family everything was black or white. There was right and there was wrong. Our home was kosher and shomer Shabbos. We didn't use electricity or drive on the Sabbath. I went to a Jewish day school. I don't remember the precise issue but my father once said to me, "You have to do it this way because these are the rules of the house." And I said, "What if I don't want to do it this way?" He said, "Then you don't have to live here." I said, "Well, I don't want to do it this way." He said, "Let's go upstairs and pack your bags." I was only five or six years old. By the time he got out my little duffel bag and put my clothes in it, we didn't need to go any further. The message was clear.

A big issue with me in high school was what time I got to synagogue. My father wanted me there early, and I wanted to sleep in. We reached a defacto compromise, but there were still boundaries that I knew could not be crossed. I started putting on tefillin before morning prayers at day school.

This is a ritual most boys begin six months before their bar mitzvah. I don't really have a memory of sitting down with my dad and talking about tefillin. But it was something that I just did every morning. My father has always been proud to remind me that he has put on tefillin every day since his bar mitzvah, never missing once.

From a very early age my father's message that I was going to marry someone Jewish was unequivocal. I'd ask, "What would happen if I married somebody who wasn't Jewish?" He would sometimes joke and say, "I'd break both your arms and your legs!" His real answer was, "I don't know what I would do, but I can tell you that our relationship would never be the same." When I was 17 I went out on a date with a beautiful blond girl. We went to the movies and then for ice-cream. The next morning my father walks into my room and asks, "I heard you were out with a blonde last night. Who was she?" He had already been to morning minyan and someone there had seen us. My father was checking me out. (Actually, she was Jewish.)

Our family life was not just about rules. I was taught that we are carriers of a wonderful, ancient tradition that continues

to be relevant today, and that Judaism is a conduit for preserving family and community values and for performing acts of tzedakah and tikkun olam. This is a message that my father not only successfully communicated to me, but also to hundreds of his congregants, many of whom found renewed meaning in their Judaism. He taught by example. He spearheaded the Soviet Jewry movement in Milwaukee. In the 1970s he led demonstrations. We often had Russian immigrants in our home for Passover. My father had a Russian Haggadah so he would have them read it and then discuss the Passover experience.

In an almost shepherd-like way, my father has always expressed a true love for K'lal Yisrael—the Jewish People. With every new Jew he meets, he can't help but ask about their family, their origins, their community, their rabbi—as if to place them in his mind into the greater Jewish community that he so cherishes. And when he comes across Jews in trouble—strangers, he obsesses until he can find a way to somehow help solve their problems. After my father retired from the pulpit, he relocated to Miami but continues his work. He helps immigrants get visas, helps with housing and job placement, and continues to provide spiritual guidance to Israeli and Russian families, sometimes even teaching bar mitzvah to their children. He leads community-wide High Holiday services for unaffiliated Jews, I'm sure with the hope that his words might in some way encourage them to strengthen their bonds to K'lal Yisrael. As Jews I believe, like my father, that we have much to teach the world about charity, decency, and human values. I am trying to raise my children in much the same way my parents raised me.

On Shabbat my son Nadiv and I go to synagogue together for shacharit, the morning service. He carries a soft stuffed toy

Torah. When they open the ark to take out the Torah, he goes up on the bimah. He stands perfectly still, almost in awe. Its very moving for me to watch. He follows the men when they walk with the Torah. I'm teaching him about sitting in synagogue, the same way that my father taught me. On Shabbat afternoon, we will go for a hike in the woods near our house. We make up stories and songs. When my children go to sleep I teach the Shema. "Hear, oh Israel, the Lord our God, the Lord is one. Blessed be his glorious kingdom forever and ever." We sing the paragraph, "V'ahavta" That's what my father did with me. ■

Sam Heller of Bethesda, Maryland is a retired government economist and World War II veteran. He has three children and two grandchildren.

SAM HELLER

The streets raised me. All five of us kids grew up in a railroad flat in Hell's Kitchen, New York. My parents didn't want us to get in trouble, but they had a store that was open from seven in the morning to midnight. My father worked hard, but my poor mother worked day and night. Never had a social life. In frustration she would say "'Imglikn hobn mir, nisht kein kinder.' I had misfortunes, not kids." I revered her.

We were quiet kids. We were little Jewish boys in a mostly non-Jewish neighborhood. I got harassed occasionally, called "Jewboy." My older brother got picked on by some kids he knew. Threw him down, took his money and made him cry. Same people who were friends later on in life. We never brought this kind of stuff to my father's attention.

I was very much involved with my kids and their education. I diapered them as babies. I wiped them. I raised my kids. I love my kids! I didn't just leave it to my wife. I found all the colleges for them. I used to go over to the American College of Education and look up colleges. Knowing the SAT achievements of my kids, I didn't believe all this schmaltz about how you had to go to a particular college. I said, just get a degree, nobody gives a damn where you to college. If you're an accountant, the government will take you right away if you get enough points.

I always thought it was important to study. I went to college at night. I was determined to get a degree. That was a step in coming into the world as a full-blown educated human being. To say I was a college graduate. The kind of person who had a degree was not going to be in a tenement.

Before I was married I was very self-conscious that I wasn't getting anywhere economically. It was the Depression so I wasn't doing well. I was literally a failure economically. I finally got a job with the Federal Government. Then war broke out and I was in the Army five years, New Guinea and the Philippines. I was in the Medical Department. After the war I stayed in the reserves. Got to be a colonel.

I was 50 years with my wife. A lot of people don't make it that long. What made it work? Love, L O V E. You believe in love? I've still got all her love letters. I'm a romantic.

I love to go on cruises with my oldest daughter. Mediterranean. Greece. Turkey. Portugal. Casablanca. I meet people. I am a quipster, quick-witted, a shmoozer. I love it. Love luxury. Because I didn't grow up in it.

What I'm most proud of is that I helped raise my kids They're all very loveable. I just want them to be happy and get happily married.

And the advice I give to other fathers—"Enjoy!" ■

Jeffrey Cohen and his wife, Arlene, live near Detroit with their twins, Joshua and Allison. The children have fragile X syndrome, a genetic condition which causes a range of learning disabilities. Jeffrey and his wife are on the board of directors of the National Fragile X Foundation, which helps raise awareness, supports research, and provides assistance to other affected families.

JEFFREY COHEN

My father taught me to be responsible in life. His father was a tailor from Russia who was in and out of financial trouble and at times could not provide for his family. As a result my father had to go to work at a very young age.

When I was growing up, he worked for the *Detroit Free Press* and made sure that the newspapers were on the streets by 5:00 each morning. It was a hard life and he'd often ask for my help. I look back on those times, driving around the city all night, as a time we could really talk. Seeing him work so hard inspired me to go to college and to become a professional.

I met my wife at Wayne State University in Detroit. On our first date she fell down some stairs and twisted her ankle. Instead of going to a fine restaurant as planned, I wheeled her into an emergency room. We married two days after I took the bar exam.

We worked very hard to start our family. Arlene had two miscarriages and it was a very sad time. We got through it by relying on each other. We were then, and remain today, good friends who can always talk to one another.

We sought genetic counseling and got a clean bill of health. However, our plans for a family stalled and a fertility work-up followed. We remained strong and met this next challenge as a team. I was present for each office visit and even gave Arlene the required injections each night. Her resulting pregnancy came about through some pretty advanced science but I was

with her every step of the way. Arlene said it best, "You should at least be in the room when your wife gets pregnant."

Within a few weeks she had an ultrasound. As we watched the screen together, she held up two fingers. The technician looked at us and confirmed that it was twins. We were completely blown away. It was like the world was made right again, two miscarriages and now twins. Their birth was breathtaking. It was the most amazing thing to see those two little lives come into the world.

After six months Arlene felt that something just wasn't right, particularly with our son. As I look back I see that I was in denial. I didn't want to hear that everything wasn't perfect and our pediatrician supported me. She would tell Arlene "You're overreacting, you're a first-time mother." It bothered me that Arlene kept pushing the issue. I just wanted to be happy with our beautiful young family. However, the kids missed milestones in their development. My son sat up and crawled late but then a month later he was walking. Things weren't obvious—at least not to me.

But Arlene knew that something wasn't right. More tests, more specialists, and it seemed as though we had ruled out every syndrome known to man. That is except one, something called "fragile X syndrome". We didn't do that test. The doctor explained "Your son is too high functioning. Kids with fragile X are retarded." More support for my denial.

It wasn't until the kids were four years old that we finally got the confirmation. One pediatrician finally said, "This is the last test we can do, a simple blood test. Let's get it out of the way. I'm sure it will be negative." So we did the test for fragile X and it was positive.

At the time the only published literature available was based on studies of the most significantly affected individuals, so the initial information was quite bleak. The next day Arlene and I went to a local medical school library and read everything we could get our hands on. We were sitting at two different tables, each with our own stack of articles, each crying quietly. We looked up from our tears and saw each other, then moved and sat together, still crying.

We kept reading, looking for something positive, but there was next to nothing. We experienced the diagnosis in much the same way as a death in the family, not in the physical sense, but as in the death of our dreams. I knew that my kids were not going to die, but like all parents I dreamed that my children would do more with their lives than I did. My father was a working class man who did not go to college and here I am a lawyer. I had the same dream for my kids. That dream was so alive and so vibrant on the day they were born, but with the diagnosis, that all came crashing down around me.

When we first learned about fragile X we decided not to tell anyone. Our kids were going to have their differences, but we were not going to put a name on it. We were afraid that a label would be misused by others to their detriment. Then we attended a conference sponsored by the National Fragile X Foundation. The experience changed our minds about keeping fragile X a secret. It was like a fog had lifted. We received useful and positive information and we wanted to share our experience and help others. We learned that children with fragile X are very capable of learning, but have a unique learning style. We went public with family, friends, and schools so that our kids could get the help they needed to succeed. We co-authored "Our Journey from Personal Seclusion to Full Inclusion." That was the beginning of our healing, our journey back to happiness. Grateful for the transformation, we joined the board of directors of the National Fragile X Foundation. Two years later I was elected president.

It's been ten years since that day in the library. Now I understand that although there are things that are difficult for my kids, they are unique individuals who have strengths and weaknesses like everyone else. The dreams I had for them that day in the delivery room are not gone, they've just changed. My dream for my children is qualitatively no less than before; that they live happy, productive, and independent lives, that they have friends and find others to love and build relationships with and that they remain connected to a Jewish community.

Over the years I have grown philosophically dedicated to educational inclusion and classroom diversity. Each year I speak to both kids' classes on the importance of respecting and celebrating the things that make us each unique.

My daughter is now in ninth grade. She is an accomplished author and painter. My son is in eighth grade, enjoys classic rock and roll and loves connecting with people. Both are fully included in all aspects of public and religious school. Last year they successfully chanted their Torah portions and the blessings at their B'nai Mitzvah. Our hearts soared with pride.

Although I was a rebellious youth, I was fortunate to remain connected to a wonderful Jewish congregation. I stayed in religious school through the twelfth grade and belong to that same congregation today. The rabbi that officiated at my parents' wedding officiated at my wedding and at my children's B'nai Mitzvah. He often spoke to me about joining the rabbinate. As a teen I would have absolutely no part of it. When I told him I'd be attending law school he said I was "wasting my talents."

I often wonder whether he was right. I have come to realize, that second only to the love I have for my wife and kids, that what gives me the greatest satisfaction in life is helping others. I am blessed that this is a passion I share with Arlene and it has truly made our marriage stronger. Not a day goes by that we don't take calls from families around the country trying to cope. We lecture in schools, national conferences, at medical colleges, and lobby in Washington. While I truly enjoy the practice of law, the real joy that I get out of life comes from helping others in crisis turn their lives around and helping them and their kids survive and learn to see the glass of life as half-full and not half-empty.

While that may not address the religious component of what a rabbi does, that's pretty much how I see the job description. I think of that rabbi often and know that he was right about me all along. It continues to give me great pride and a real sense of inner peace.

For more information about fragile X syndrome contact the National Fragile X Foundation at 800 688-8765 or on the web at www.fragilex.org. ■

Cecil Alexander of Atlanta, Georgia, was a Marine dive bomber pilot in World War II and was awarded two Distinguished Flying Crosses. An honored architect, community leader, and civil rights activist, he chaired the Atlanta Citizens Advisory Committee for Urban Renewal, is on the board of the Martin Luther King Jr. Center, and received the Whitney Young Award. A widower, he and his wife jointly share eight children and thirteen grandchildren. In 2001 he redesigned the Georgia State Flag.

CECIL ALEXANDER

I think my values have influenced my children. My youngest son just got off the City Council after serving two terms. I remember telling him, "You know, Doug, you've got one big handicap in politics." He asked me, "What's that?" I told him, "You're honest."

The first Alexander that I know of came to Charleston, South Carolina about 1760. He was the reader in the Sephardic congregation Beth El Elohim. He was a traditionalist and fought changes in the rituals eliminating Spanish from the service. He served in the Continental Army during the Revolutionary War. His grandson, Aaron, migrated to Atlanta in 1847. In 1866, after the Civil War, my grandfather and his brother opened a store, the J.M. Alexander Hardware Company. My father inherited it.

My father was a distinguished gentleman. If you'd gone to central casting to get a senator, you'd have picked out Cecil Alexander Sr. He was raised in the Southern tradition but never said anything offensive to a black person, but he expected them to stay in their place. Atlanta was totally segregated as I was growing up. It took me a long time to realize that it was wrong.

Our family belonged to The Temple in Atlanta but my father was not religious. Yet, he never let any anti-Semitic slur go by without reacting vigorously to it; he was really a tiger. I'm sure it had an influence on me, that I never would let anything pass either.

I worked in the family store as a teenager during the Depression and nobody had money. People came in and bought maybe half a dozen nails. I'll never forget when my father finally closed the store. After the war, his lease ran out and he couldn't get another store. He closed it in 1947. So, my father wrote me a check to help me get started in my career. I had just started my architectural practice. I remember my father breaking down and sobbing when he did that. I think he felt overwhelmed closing down the business his father had started in 1866.

My first attraction to architecture was motivated by living in a neighborhood that was under construction. I scrounged wood to build a clubhouse. At the time I wanted to go to art school. My father said, "Oh no, I don't want you to be a starving artist." He didn't realize you could be a starving architect with a lot more responsibility than an artist has. So I went to Yale and then MIT but World War II started.

Before I joined the military I had obtained a commercial pilot's license. About that time I met a German couple who had escaped and described the situation in Germany. From that time on I lost all interest in school. I wanted to go fight Germans. I went into the Navy and then the Marines.

I ended up fighting the Japanese. I became a dive bomber. You're going down at a 70 degree angle, a real test of flying ability, nerves, and your ability to hit the target. I've always been thankful that I was in the central Pacific and not bombing cities.

After the war I completed my studies at Harvard. The instructors there were from the German Bauhaus; Walter Gropius, Marcel Breuer. None of these fine architects had commissions because it was right after the war, so they were all focused on teaching. I started a firm with others and relocated back to Atlanta.

Through my involvement with the business community I became involved with the Civil Rights Movement in Atlanta. I've always thought that the friendships that existed in Atlanta across racial lines evolved because many of the men in power had practically been raised by black women. In some cases, there was more love there than there was between mother and son. One group that's never gotten the recognition it deserves in the Civil Rights Movement in Atlanta is the women. They did and said things their husbands couldn't, or wouldn't. They integrated the restaurants. They went around to all the restaurants and told the owners, "We'll back you. We'll come." And they did. They stuck it out.

During the early days of the Civil Rights Movement a black minister said, "The reason Atlanta is different is, there are black folks, and there're white folks, but the money's all green." I always felt that the Atlanta business community hid behind money and finances. But they also knew damn well there was something wrong with segregation, and that we needed to correct it for reasons other than money. So, I became kind of a conduit between the business and black community, to solve issues.

I was president of the Atlanta chapter of the American Institute of Architects. The urban renewal effort here in Atlanta was floundering. Mayor Hartsfield really didn't like the idea of urban renewal and he hadn't done anything about it, but the business community kept pushing him. It started out there were only seven of us: two women, two blacks, and three white men. Many issues came before us that did not directly relate to urban renewal, such as boycotts and integration. I later became the chairman of the Housing Resources Committee, with a charge of developing 17,000 low income housing units. I was helping developers get through all the red tape and rezoning. I got to know the black community very, very well.

I was always getting into trouble. My kids grew up seeing Daddy on TV and reading about me in the newspapers. During all of this the Klan was active. I got a call at the house one evening, and the guy says, "Is that you on the tube wanting to move niggers here?" I said, "Well, I haven't been looking at television, but it could be." He said, "My name is so-and-so, and I live at so-and-so," which was very close by. "I'm a former agent in the FBI, and I want you to know you're a traitor to the United States of America." I replied "I'm a retired Marine lieutenant colonel with combat experience, and I resent what you say." And I hung up. I'd gotten a lot of threats by phone, and sometimes down at city hall, face-to-face. I didn't pay attention to most of them, because people didn't identify themselves. But this guy identified himself. So I went out and I bought an automatic. He probably could have outshot me, being an FBI man, but it was a very funny feeling having a gun in the house. Luckily, I never heard anything more from that guy.

The most interesting dinner I had with Martin Luther King Jr. was after The Temple was bombed. Rabbi Rothchild had invited King and his wife to come to dinner at their home. He invited my wife and me as well. We got there and King was locked up in jail down in Albany. In the middle of the dinner, King showed up. Since then I have thought that one of the best, most iron-clad excuses for not being on time for dinner is "I'm in jail."

In 1993 I became concerned about the image Atlanta was going to have during the Olympics. The black community was threatening to boycott. I thought it would help if we changed the state flag. I designed a flag which I thought compromised on the concerns of everyone. Across the bottom was a ribbon of flags that had flown over Georgia since pre-colonial times: the French, the Spanish, the English, the American Revolution, the original Confederate flag—not the Cross of Saint Andrews—and the U.S. flag. At some point I was in an elevator with the governor. I told him, "Governor, I've got a flag here that I'd like to show you, that I think is a compromise." When he got off the elevator, he says, "I like you, Cecil, but I don't want anything to do with that flag." But an attorney named Joe Beck (whose father was a model for Atticus Finch in "To Kill a Mockingbird") got real interested in it.

We talked to some members of the legislature and got some lukewarm support. In April of 2000 we finally had a ten-minute appointment with Governor Barnes. Joe and I went in there. The governor said, "This may be the alternative I've been looking for." We didn't hear anything more about it for quite some time.

The American Jewish Committee here was pushing for a change in the flag. I asked them if I could bring my flag to one of their meetings. A black state legislator who had been pushing for the flag to change for years was at the meeting. When my flag was passed around, I recall a rabbi saying, "This will never fly." However, the legislator asked me to show it once again to the governor.

The morning that the governor finally signed the bill they raised the new flag over the Capitol, I was out in front. There wasn't a big crowd, but the state legislator was there with a big grin on his face. He ran over and gave me a hug. Laughing, he said, "The week before I saw you at the meeting, I was with the governor, and he said, 'We're going to go with Alexander's flag.' But he swore me to secrecy. I couldn't say anything there that day. It was all I could do to keep from grinning or kicking you under the table."

I got a hell of a thrill out of it when they raised my flag. I was weeping. ▪

Stuart Eizenstat of Chevy Chase, Maryland, served as President Carter's chief Domestic Affairs advisor, as the U.S. Ambassador to the European Union, and as Under Secretary of Commerce during the Clinton era. He successfully negotiated major agreements with the Swiss, Germans, Austrians, and French regarding Holocaust restitution issues, described in his book Imperfect Justice: Looted Assets, Slave Labor, and the Unfinished Business of World War II, *He is married to Frances Eizenstat, and has two sons and four grandchildren.*

STUART EIZENSTAT

My grandfather came from Russia to Atlanta. He grew up in Atlanta in the early days of Coca Cola. My father told me a story that when he was a boy, there was a knock on the door, and my grandfather, who spoke mostly Yiddish, was engaged in discussion with a well-dressed man at the door. My father said, in Yiddish, "What is this all about?" And he said, "It was just a man selling something." He said, "What was he trying to sell?" "Stock in Coca Cola." "Well, Tateh, why don't you buy any?" He replied, "No one will ever drink colored water!" So we've always said, "Well, if you'd only bought one share of stock." But the broader impact he had was when he decided, at the age of 80-plus, to make aliyah to Israel. My father, uncle, aunt, and his children said, "You're crazy at your age to go to Israel." He said he wanted to die in the Holy Land. My first trip to Israel was in 1965 and I saw him about six months before he died, in an old-age home in Petach Tikvah. It was very emotional for me to have that connection to Israel. Now, fast-forward to 1981. After I'd finished the Carter White House, my wife and I were invited by Prime Minister Begin to be official guests of the government, to thank me for the help I'd given to Israel. I made a trip to visit my grandfather's grave and discovered something quite startling. I discovered that his father, my great-grandfather, was buried only a row away,

something I hadn't known. He had clearly wanted to be buried next to his father. He never said that to any of his children. We have gone through every conceivable record in Israel to see what story there was about my great-grandfather, but we have never been able to discover it. Our assumption is that when my grandfather left Russia in 1904 for Atlanta, that his father made a path to Palestine. It gives me a very powerful connection to the State of Israel to know that both my grandfather and great-grandfather are buried there.

My father had a major impact on me. He was as close to being a Biblical scholar as a layman can be. One of my very strong memories was that on Friday nights, he would take out his Chumash in Hebrew, with the Rashi interpretation, and he would read and explain the portion of the week. That's a tradition I've carried on with my children.

From my father I got a sense of Jewish traditions, the importance of learning, the importance of what messages the Bible had for our current life. From my mother I learned to respect people of all kinds. She came from Chicago, so she didn't have the racial hang-ups people had in segregated Atlanta. One of my early memories of confronting injustice is one I failed. It gave me a perspective almost on those who grew up in Germany during the Holocaust, how easy it is to accept the accepted order, even when it's unjust. I was coming back from synagogue on the bus, sitting at the rear of the whites-only section. An elderly black lady came on laden with bags, and I remember struggling with whether I should give her my seat. Every instinct was that I should get up and let her sit, yet I couldn't break with the mores of the time and let her sit in the white section, which would also have been a violation of the law. My mother really helped sensitize me to injustices like this.

My folks sent me to Camp Blue Star, a magnet camp for Jews in the South, and had my first taste of politics when I was drafted to be mayor of "Teenage Village". I got very involved in basketball and ended up becoming All-City and Honorable Mention All-American in Atlanta. I was the third leading scorer in the city my senior year. I've always said it should be with an asterisk, because it's pre-integration.

The concept of tikkun olam had a role in my interest in public life. I majored in political science at the University of North Carolina and got to serve as a congressional intern. That catalyzed my interest in public service and politics. I was in the Johnson White House, the Carter White House, and the Clinton administration. I very much brought my Jewish values and my Jewish views, but in a way that I've always thought was important to distinguish. If I had been the Jewish adviser to Carter, or the Jewish representative on Holocaust negotiations for Clinton, or the Jewish ambassador to the E.U., I would have been discounted. I was the domestic policy adviser to Carter who happened to be Jewish. We worked 80 hours a week at the White House, but everybody knew I left early Friday night. When I was in Brussels as ambassador to the E.U., my wife, Fran, and I kept a kosher residence. Yet it was important that I was always seen, and saw myself, as a representative of the

United States of America. During the very difficult Holocaust negotiations, had I been seen as the Jewish advocate, I could not have mediated these suits and gotten eight billion dollars worth of settlements from the Swiss, German, Austrian, and French companies. We wanted to help victims, both Jewish and non-Jewish. I had to be viewed as someone who wanted to maintain our foreign and economic relations with the countries and the companies being sued. That is not an easy balancing act. I feel like I have as many scars from the representatives of the Jewish survivor groups who wanted me to be more of an advocate for them as I do from the foreign companies and governments.

Politics and diplomacy are very different. I was President Carter's chief domestic adviser. I had expected that after Clinton was elected that I'd get some domestic job. The job that came open was Ambassador to the European Union. Instead of negotiating with senators and congressmen, I was negotiating with foreign governments. I learned how foreigners look at the United States, how much the United States means to the world. Later I became Undersecretary of Commerce and Undersecretary of State and began the Holocaust negotiations. I did the Kyoto global warming accords and negotiated major agreements with the European Union on Helms-Burton and the Iran and Libya Sanctions Act. To be a good negotiator, you have to understand what the other side's bottom line is for their constituency. And you've got to understand what your bottom line is for your constituency. And it's finding that very narrow line.

There are some relationships between parenting and diplomacy. It sensitizes you to how kids look at things, to try to be tolerant of their views and still to try to shape those views. There's a delicate balance when you're a parent between conveying your views, your values, your ethics, transmitting L'Dor V'dor, from generation to generation, and yet allowing individuality within the parameters that you have tried to set. I've found out that you learn as much from your children as you impart to them.

There are several things in my career that have meant the most. There's nothing like the incredible experience of working in the White House. All the problems in the world converge there. Every word, every phrase, every bill, every proposal has major impacts on history. It's an unusual sensation, and one you have to make sure doesn't go to your head.

My most important accomplishment is helping Holocaust victims. Getting insurance paid, art returned. Eight billion dollars in reparations for slave and forced laborers. Uncovering the truth about the level of confiscation and theft, and helping people 50 years after the event who wouldn't have been helped. It was extremely difficult.

There's a lesson that I've learned. Respect the people who work under you as well as those who are above you. Never let your power or your title go to your head. Keep your values. Remember where you came from. Treat people as if you never had these positions. And that, to me, is all very much a part of my upbringing. ▪

Richard Joel is the president of Yeshiva University in New York. For many years he was the president of Hillel, the Jewish college student organization. A former New York assistant district attorney, he and his wife, Esther, have six children. This interview was conducted in Jerusalem.

I grew up in a home full of love. If I am not a good guy today, I have no excuses. My father taught me a Yiddish expression "If it doesn't work with good and it doesn't work with bad, make it work with good."

I learned from my father to be strong enough to be sensitive. I learned that Jewishness is a natural part of our being, like the air we breathe. He loved to play Yiddish folk songs and share his joy.

He became ill about the time of my bar mitzvah. During the service he had the third aliyah. He said the blessing, and broke down crying. He had a brain tumor. Five months later he died at home in my mother's arms.

His death contributed to my faith in God and in a world after death. I still talk to my father every day. The final gift that my father gave me is the awareness that I'm going to die and that life is to be savored. Since the act of living is a pleasure and an adventure; sharing that with children makes you richer.

My wife, Esther, and I are very much in love. We believe that life is about giving and sharing. If a child behaves badly we do not say, "You are bad," we tell them "What you did was very disappointing to me." There has to be discipline, boundaries and consistency. I want my children to understand that the world doesn't revolve around them, but that they are critically important players. I want them to believe that they are capable of dignity and graciousness.

I am a role model not just for my own children but in my work with students. Hillel is responsible for helping Jewish college students to experience their Jewishness as valuable. Most Jewish young people do not really understand this. Most have never had a "Jewish WOW moment." Hillel's mission is a Jewish Rennaissance. Jews are part of a great story and it's time to reinvigorate it by helping each generation take ownership. We engage and empower Jewish students to become involved with their Jewish journey.

I think it's important to teach Jewish students how to represent Israel at a time when it's under siege. On missions to Israel, we expose them to the issues and teach them serious advocacy skills. Since the breakout of suicide-bombings and the collapse of the peace talks, we have redoubled our efforts.

Torah means a world of values and love of family and community. It's the concentric circles of intimacy that make up life. At some point my kids will say Kaddish for me. The eternity that I build is how I raise my children.

Mitch Levine is an obstetrician-gynecologist living in a communal house in Lincoln, Massachusetts. He is married to Sarah and has a young daughter, Miriam, with her, and a teenaged daughter, Elizabeth, from a previous marriage.

My father was a pediatrician. My grandfather was an Orthodox rabbi. My grandparents lived with us when I was growing up. I would go downstairs and study Talmud with my grandfather. I earned my first dollar for memorizing ten pages of Talmud for him.

I went away to Yale in 1969. There was a lot going on. There were the Black Panthers, hippies, and revolutionaries from all over the country. I'd led a somewhat sheltered life, so meeting all these people and trying these interesting ideas was very eye-opening.

I remained traditional in some ways. I was part of the kosher kitchen at Yale but I also was experimenting with people of all different cultures. I hitchhiked cross-country to visit a friend who lived in a redwood forest and had lots of adventures on the way. I'm sure my mother died a thousand deaths while I hitchhiked.

I had always wanted to be a doctor. While in medical school, I again came across people with very different viewpoints. I had a friend who was into alternative health. She told me about using different colors for healing. I would tell my fellow residents and doctors about these things. One night I was in the emergency room and a guy came in with a gunshot wound. We operated on him for six hours and we were all covered with red blood. The chief resident turned to me and goes, "So, Mitch, do you think blue would help?"

I came to Harvard for my residency, a very traditional place. I started to question a lot of things. A lot of the

C-sections that were done were unnecessary. I started to hang out with midwives who were doing homebirths, and provided consultation and back-up to them. Some of the doctors had Caesarean rates of 50 or 60 percent. One week I took a couple of the C-sections that the attending doctors had done and presented them as my own. I said, "Well, the woman came in in labor and she was four centimeters and several hours later, she was seven centimeters… and then at 5:00, I did a C-section." They exclaimed, "Why'd you do a C-section? That's terrible!" I let everybody say this. Then I said, "Actually they weren't my cases. They were the attending doctors' cases." So really by the end of the residency, I wasn't really sure where I was going to fit in. There was a certain lack of ethics in medicine.

I'd been going to the Rainbow Gathering of all the different alternative people from all over. I met up with Dr. Patch Adams there. I went to the medical tent to see if I could help. Here was a doctor who was six foot five, with long braids and a red clown's nose, doing his healing with love and laughter. I saw people doing all different kinds of healing; acupuncture, homeopathy, naturopathy, crystal healing, all very different from my Harvard background. This was wonderful to me. I traveled with Patch and lived in different spiritual communities. I learned a lot about true healing as opposed to just technical medicine. When I came back to Boston I opened an alternatively-oriented practice. I was interested in doing homebirths and in people healing themselves. I couldn't find other doctors who wanted to do births the way I did, but the midwives did, so I partnered with them.

Birth is the most profound moment in the mother's and baby's life. I've learned so much from people's magnificence, their courage at births. Once I delivered a baby that was not breathing, was essentially dead when it was born. I immediately started mouth-to-mouth resuscitation and was looking into the baby's eyes. After a few minutes the baby revived, and the mother asked "is my baby going to be damaged?" I said, "Absolutely not." I knew with absolute surety from looking in the baby's eyes as I was breathing into his mouth that the baby was fine. And the baby was fine.

We really encouraged fathers. They need the reassurance that their presence is important, that it's really helpful to their wife. I let them know they won't mess up or faint. Most of them are very loving and supportive to their wives. Part of birth is being able to relax and open. You have to feel really safe and supported to do that. Who could possibly be better to love and encourage the wife during labor? I think having the husband there is crucial. And then there's the joy of being there when the baby is born, of greeting the baby.

I got to be at the birth of both of my children at home. I delivered baby Miriam myself. Sarah was in labor for 35 hours. Her parents were there, and my 14-year-old daughter, Elizabeth, was hugging and massaging Sarah and breathing with her. In the early part of the labor people came and drummed. Sarah was so magnificent and courageous and strong and joyful through the birth. Miriam was born in our bed under the chuppah that we got married under. It's a very beautiful thing to share.

The other thing is death. I think people often die in the hospital in a very sterile, unsupportive, unloving, environment. It would be great if more people could die at home surrounded by their family and loved ones. My grandparents both got to die at home, because my parents took care of them till the end, and they were very traditional, old-world Jewish people. They would have been so miserable in the hospital. My grandmother, who lived to 93, died at home with my mother there and one of her granddaughters holding her hand. That should be the way to die as well as to birth.

For some time I was a single parent after the end of my first marriage. Elizabeth spent half the time with me and half with her mom. I did that for a number of years, and then decided I wanted more family, so I got together with other people who also had kids and other single people and couples, and we made a big group home. We had people from all different races, religions, backgrounds, and all lived together. Now I have the actual traditional wife and child, but for many years, we had an alternative family with other people who were single-parenting and other single people and couples. In some ways this is the first traditional family thing I've done. I'm actually married and we have a baby. I think my teenage daughter gets a big kick out of that.

I have a men's group that's been meeting for 16 years at the house. Sarah has a women's group. We've had co-counseling workshops, dance workshops, breathing workshops. One of our housemates is a Buddhist monk. Everybody has their own space. Sometimes I retreat up to my room and close the door, but I also love coming down to the kitchen and just hanging out with other people too.

I brought Elizabeth to P'nai Or, a Jewish renewal group. I've talked to her quite a bit about Jewish stuff. I've given her books to read like *Exodus* and *Mila 18*. For her bat mitzvah we visited Israel, where a lot of my family lives.

What I'm really proud of Elizabeth is that she's a gentle, thoughtful, considerate person, very loving. She's really an amazing kid, with deep understanding and sensitivity. She talks to me about everything, about issues around sexuality and drugs and peer interactions, how to dress, and how people interact with each other in school. I'm very grateful for that. I think trusting your kids and letting them make their own choices is what gives them the smarts, the strength, and the will to make good choices. If you're always trying to control them they never get to make their own choices.

I love being a doctor. I'm very grateful to have that as my work. When we are out in Cambridge or anywhere we go, people come by with their 18-year-old son and say, "This is the baby that you delivered!" When we were in Jerusalem we were on Ben Yehudah Street, and a woman came up to me with her with her 40-year-old daughter and said, "This is the daughter that your father delivered." It was so sweet. My father had been her pediatrician. As much as I've lived this totally alternative way, we have lived much the same story. He was totally devoted to his work and to his family. I think that sense of responsibility is probably what I learned from him.

David Zabarsky is the owner of Martek Instruments, which designs and manufactures equipment for ultrapure water analysis. A former Marine officer, he lives in Raleigh, North Carolina with his wife, Stacey, and three children.

DAVID ZABARSKY

My father stressed family and education. High school bored me, college was an intellectual awakening. When I decided to go to UCLA, Dad suggested I check out ROTC. I was accepted as a Marine option, which appealed to my sense of adventure and duty.

I became an infantry officer. You train your men to survive on the battlefield, how to set up fields of fire, how to ambush. I had Latinos, African-Americans, and Filipinos in my platoon, people from all walks of life. As a new lieutenant I was thrust into this environment with tremendous responsibility.

When I first held my first child in my arms everything I had done up to that point, including the Marine Corps, paled in significance. I desire for all of my children, but especially my son, to serve their country, preferably in the Marine Corps.

I'm a strict disciplinarian and my children know exactly where it is I'm coming from. A lot of Jewish families do not discipline their children enough, and then wonder why their kids act up. I love my children dearly and am following a way that will help them survive in this world.

I tell my older daughter, Jessica, "Teach your boyfriend to come in, look me straight in the eye, introduce himself, and shake my hand as hard as he can. That's what worked for me. Don't shuffle your feet. Go straight to the man of the house, shake his hand, introduce yourself. Compliment the mom, and ask what time to bring the girl home." I've told Jessica, "There's no way we can stop you from being sexually active. The message I give to you is, be responsible." She's not allowed to date single dates until she's 16. There's been a couple of instances where she's wanted to go out, and we won't allow that, because of the driver. She says, "Why not?" I say, "When you're driving, that's not a problem. I know you." We have a rule in this family. It's called 'house rules'. You live here, you live by the rules.

If they want to get a laugh out of me, all they have to do is ask for allowance. "If you want to do a particular job, I'm willing to pay you, that's another story." When everything is handed to you, what does it mean? I want my children to be contributing members of society.

I drove with my son up to North Dakota and down to Louisiana on business trips. I drove to Dallas with my youngest daughter. My eldest and I went on a trip to Michigan. I teach my kids to appreciate everything they have and to ignore material things. I hope by my example that their lives can be fulfilling. I've found that helping others, making a difference, puts purpose in my own life.

When I've driven 20 hours on the road, I've had my discussions with myself and God, with how I've lived my life. I've done everything I've ever wanted to do. I wish the same for my children. My philosophy is to live every day like it's your last. At the end of the day, when it's dark out, when you're listening to the crickets, I kiss my children and wife goodnight. That is what is our religion is. ◼

Ben Stauber lives in Spartanburg, South Carolina. A successful businessman and retired Air Force officer, he and his wife have two grown children.

BEN STAUBER

I'm not a typical rabbi's son. I was seven when my father, Max, took the pulpit in Spartanburg, a sleepy Southern town. The congregation was 55 families if you counted everybody. My Jewish friends here were like cousins. They meant a lot, because I could feel comfortable and feel normal around them. This was a very Christian town growing up.

He was from a long line of rabbis. His father was a chocham, a wise man. The remarkable thing about my dad was, the better you got to know him, the more you ended up loving and respecting him. He was a man of so few flaws. The man had a heart of gold.

When you're a kid, people ask, "What does your dad do?" Being a rabbi's son, right away they knew I was Jewish. I was different in a positive way. There was a great deal of respect for my family because of my father's position and the way he carried himself. I had many different friends. They knew not to smoke in the house on Shabbos. They loved chopped liver and our seder, they knew the birkat…these are my Christian friends.

I never went to a high school football game because they were on Friday night. We would come home, have a big Shabbos dinner, then pull out the books, Rashi and others, and we'd study. I wanted to be outside playing football with my buddies. That was tough.

My father and I would drive to a farm and get crates of chickens, and he would shecht them. And he was a mohel. Growing up with my father was like having God's personal representative in the house. He was almost magical. People loved my folks, to that extent where they could just walk in

and be welcome. My father reminded me, "You're the rabbi's son. You have to behave." Being a rebellious child, I used to say "You're the rabbi, not me." But I absolutely respected him. We were poor as church mice. We never missed a meal, because I think 90 percent of my parents' income went to food. We were feeding everybody. He said, "It's not about money." He watched young kids grow up and he married them. And then he brissed their kids. And he buried them.

I finished college and joined the Air Force so I wouldn't go to Vietnam but ended up going anyway. I was in an air rescue squadron. He was very proud of what I did in the service. He was a staunch American patriot. Interestingly, when I went to Vietnam, he started counseling young men on conscientious objector status. My mother lit another candle every Shabbos, so I'd make it home safely. When the Vietnam Memorial was dedicated I wept. I couldn't believe that finally somebody said something nice about the guys that put their ass on the line.

Raising my own kids every Friday night we had Shabbos. When other kids had Christmas trees we had Hanukkah decorations, and dressed them up for Purim. My son's talking about being a rabbi! Which makes me happier than I can ever tell you. My daughter knows how important it is to find the right person, hopefully Jewish, and to have a family. That their mother converted makes it plausible for them. We have a warm, loving family, and the usual pulls and tugs and problems, so it's never dull in our house! ◼

Simms Taback lives in Willow, New York. He and his wife, Gail, have a blended family of three grown children, Emily, Lisa, and Jason. His book Joseph and the Overcoat, *based on a Yiddish folksong, won a Caldecott Medal in 2000, the premier award for illustrated children's books.*

SIMMS TABACK

I drew at a very early age. I went to WPA art classes, the 1930s program started by the New Deal. I had an arts and crafts teacher in Camp Kinderland, a Jewish socialist summer camp, who encouraged me.

My dad was a communist. We were always going to protest marches. My father would quote Marx. He didn't talk in terms of values. When I was a teenager, I started to have political disagreements with him. To him religion was an anathema, except for Passover, when we went to my grandmother's on the Lower East Side. For years I thought, "This is a holiday where Jewish families get together and argue." When my mother died I got really close with my father. We made a trip to Russia together, where he was born. But I could never get him to discuss his feelings. I think that had to do with the fact that he was an orphan and it was too heartbreaking.

I don't remember kids' books in my family. I don't think my parents knew about kids books, and they probably didn't have the money. We were pretty poor. The kids' books that I had were like *The Youth of Lenin*. I didn't read *Alice In Wonderland* until I went to college.

My first children's books came as a job. The style of my work always lent itself to doing kids' books. I did one I really liked called *Too Much Noise* adapted from a Jewish folk story. I did a number of novelty books, *Snakey Riddles*, *Fishy Riddles*. My kids were grown up when I was doing them so I had grandchildren to test them out on.

I learned the song "Joseph and the Overcoat" in Camp Kinderland and began to make it into a book. I started to put in collage elements of my family, and stuff I remembered about Yiddish culture. Yiddish was my first language. My father's in there. There's the boat that my mother came to this country on. I put a babushka on my daughter Emily. There's my grandson Sean, my granddaughter, my daughter, Lisa, and my friend Renald who's actually a black man; I turned him into a Chasid. There's my great-uncle Leibish, who adopted my father. I found old Yiddish sayings "When the coat is old, only the holes are new." I pasted them all in and colored them, and made them part of the book. I mixed everything up with Ukrainian and Polish designs, brightened it all up. Made it like I would have liked it to have been and maybe it was that way. I wanted it to feel like a lively klezmer wedding. Some people noticed that Joseph looked a lot like me.

In doing a kid's book I try to give it a look that will not just interest kids but parents too. They may have to read a book ten or fifteen times, so it's got to be interesting for adults, besides being fun for kids. The fun has to be in the way you draw the characters. I try to do it like a little animated film.

Four years before the Caldecott Award I didn't know how I was going to make a living. When you win the Caldecott, you go on the "Today Show." I get letters from schools all over the country. I answer them all. And then they send you pictures. You get all kinds! ■

Dolph Schayes, played for the Syracuse Nationals from 1949-1963, voted All National Basketball Association team 12 times. When he retired he had scored more points (19,249) than any other athlete in the game. From 1966 to 1970 he supervised the NBA referees, and in 1977 became the head coach of U.S. Maccabiah Games. With the help of his son, Dan, the U.S. team won against the Israelis 92-91 in the championship game. Dolph was elected to the Naismith Memorial Basketball Hall of Fame in 1972. Dan Schayes, an All-American at Syracuse University, was selected by the Utah Jazz in the first round of the 1981 NBA draft. A veteran of 18 seasons in the league, he also played for Denver, Los Angeles, Milwaukee, Phoenix, Miami, and Orlando.

DOLPH AND DANNY SCHAYES

Dolph: We've played 30, 40 years in major league sports, as father and son, probably a record number of years. I would have liked to have played more. You don't get tired of the game, but you get tired of the grind. If I was making like the players are today, 2, 3, 4 million dollars a year, I would have played until they ripped the uniform off me.

Danny: When I was a kid we used to do shooting games out in the driveway, playing horse and other shooting games.

Dolph: We stopped playing when Danny was able to beat me at our father-son games just when he went into college. I could see when we played one-on-one in the driveway, that Danny's strength and size were just too much for me, that his skills had become better than mine at that point.

Danny: In his era he was not only one the biggest guys in the league, but one of the biggest people in the world—6' 8" back in the 1940s was the equivalent of seven feet plus today. I remember when I was first taller than him as a sophomore in high school. That was a kind of a real mark for me, because he was a giant to me as I was growing up. Every kid wants to be taller than Dad, but with my dad, that was really something!

Dolph: I ran a basketball camp. When Danny became old enough to play he started learning fundamentals at the camp and playing competitively. Danny became strong in the fundamentals, and I think that's where he evolved his love for the game. I never imposed my will in saying, "I want you to be a basketball player, take a basketball and dribble it to school." Obviously when you're very tall you're asked to play.

Danny: There were three Jewish players in the NBA along with me: Ernie Runfeld who retired about '85, '86 and Joel Kramer, who I played with in the Maccabiah games. At first there were three, then there were two, then there was me.

Dolph: Being Jewish was never really an issue in the NBA. The NBA is a minority sport. You're there because you can play. Sports is a great equalizer: you play or you can't play and color, religion; it's just not really a big deal, because the goal is to play the game. When I came into the NBA in 1948, there were no black players. When I was learning the game in New York City, it was a Jewish sport. But in the pros it wasn't. In 1951 the first black player came into the NBA, on my team, Earl Lloyd. Before you knew it we became very integrated.

There were never any issues about black and white amongst the players. I think basketball players are somewhat more liberal. They were better educated than the baseball players, who during Hank Greenberg's time were quite anti-Semitic, and certainly anti-black. A lot of baseball players never went to college, where as in basketball, almost all the players went to college.

I started out as a schoolyard player. I played in Public School 91 and Preston Junior High School. I played in the community centers of the schools in the evenings. I learned by playing the game against good competition.

My parents came to this country from Romania in the early '20s and met in English-speaking schools. My father wrote a note to my mother, "I love you." That was the first note he ever wrote in English. The rest is history.

I knew I was Jewish. I was brought up in it. In fact, I thought the whole world was Jewish, because being in the Bronx, 90 percent of the people I lived around were Jewish. I was not bar mitzvahed, and we didn't have any traditional Jewish life. My mother didn't keep kosher, but all the food was Jewish style.

My father worked for the Consolidated Laundries company and worked his way up to manager. During the Depression, he was a cab driver. He worked hard. What I got from my father was terrific: my physical being, my body, because he was very tall, very strong. And he was a very fair-minded person. He loved sports. We used to go to baseball games at Yankee Stadium. I would enjoy bonding with him at those games.

He never really said one word or another about my playing as a kid. He was just too busy working. I played, and then, of course, he was a great fan of mine. During my college years he was at every game, and even in the pro years, he followed me all over.

Danny: When I was growing up, Dad always stressed education. He had started a business building and owned real estate. He was a great competitor as a player and hard-working as a business person. The bad news of that was that he wasn't around the house a lot. He worked long hours to put food on the table and build a business.

I grew up in a stable environment and I went to college in Syracuse, my home town. I have a degree in organic chemistry. I had a 4.0 average, an honors student. I kept playing basketball and I kept getting better and better. I was the 13th pick in the first round of the NBA draft, by Utah.

Dolph: I think what I got when I was a kid was living in an environment of study and educational competition. It was a school of middle-class, mostly Jewish kids. We had wonderful teachers that made learning fun. I think I got this love of education from the competition from the kids in school, from my peers.

There was one aspect of Danny's basketball playing that he didn't like about me; that I was a pain in the ass as a father. When I went to a game and Danny was playing, I made life miserable for the referees. I'd get up and yell at the referee. Because I was a professional I had seen the best of the game from coaching to refereeing. One time in college, a referee fouled Danny out of the game. I thought he had called several really bad fouls, just didn't know how to referee, and I stormed on the court. After I had retired from coaching I became the supervisor of referees for the league.

Danny: It was hard because I was always compared to the great Dolph Schayes, even in a small town like Syracuse. He was almost like royalty to the city. At the end of my career, I was the oldest starting player in the league. I was starting for

Orlando at 38 years old. We won a great game in Madison Square Garden. I had 21 points. Nationally televised game, in New York, you love to play in New York.

Dolph: I was the leading scorer during my career. When I retired, I had 19,500 points. I was inducted in the NBA Hall of Fame in 1972. My father was very happy about that.

There are some stand-out moments. We won a world's championship on Easter Sunday in 1955. I got 40 points one night against the Celtics, our biggest rival. A great thrill for me was not in the NBA, but coaching the 1977 U.S. entry into the Maccabiah Games. Danny was on the team. The Israeli national team had just won the European championships, but we won by one point before 10,000 people. I told the kids in the pre-game, "Fellows, we're the underdog. It's rare that a U.S. basketball team is an underdog in any game. But we're an underdog tonight, and you go show what we can do." In the last second we won off the foul line.

Danny: The Maccabiah Games is an Olympic-style event. Five thousand athletes and coaches from all over the world, all of them Jewish. The goal of the games is part sport and mostly culture. You had teams from countries with small Jewish populations that sent four or ten competitors, The United States had 230. Probably my greatest Jewish cultural experience, religious experience also, was the Maccabiah games.

Dolph: It was unbelievably exciting to see 50,000 Jews in the stadium, everybody cheering. It really enhanced the Jewish identity of our kids. It showed to them how wonderful this group of people is, that they all have the same feelings and the same will to just keep this wonderful people alive, forever.

Danny: Unlike the Olympics, it's less about sports; the cultural aspect is a key component. During one of the Maccabiah trips, I went and was bar mitzvahed on top of Masada. I was 35 or 36. It was a sunset ceremony; very lovely. Being in a Reform synagogue in the U.S. at the time was more of a social experience than a spiritual one. But once we went to Israel and got to experience the country, see the history, live the history, I made the connection that Israel was a real place, a real thing. To be there, to experience The Western Wall, a kibbutz, to see Jewish life in action, down to the presence of the military everywhere. It makes Judaism come alive. ■

Randy Rosen is a commercial realtor living in Parkland Florida. An active sports coach, he and his wife, Jacki, have two children, Jonathan and Hannah.

RANDY ROSEN

Dad was in the shmatte business. I would go with him to work in the factory. I swept floors summer after summer. When I was 14, there was a disgruntled employee he had to fire. She met him one morning coming to work. There was a scuffle, she had a gun, and he got shot. He went through surgery, needed 20 pints of blood.

That changed him. We became very close. He used to give me advice. I remember a time in tenth grade, and there was a girl that I liked a lot. She moved away, and I was crushed. I remember sitting in my room crying. He came in and talked to me, gave me advice about how to deal with it. As a teenager, you think your whole world has collapsed. But from the perspective of a father, you know that your child is going through one of those stages in life that children have to go through, where you learn life experiences. He really helped me through that moment.

He would teach me about the business, the different facets of the factory, about buyers, financial stuff, technical stuff, dealing with employees. He would guide me when I stumbled, always there to catch me. He let me be a free spirit while keeping a watchful eye. I was a good kid in high school, and I attribute a lot of that to him.

I find myself using some of the same kind of strategies with my own kids. I very much have an eye on the future. When children are born, it's a blank canvas. You have to mold and shape them, we are very concerned about helping them turn out to be good-hearted people.

Jacki and I have chosen to make the children our number one priority. I want to be with my kids. I volunteer at the JCC, where the kids are in day school. Jonathan walks through the hallway, and right in front of all his friends and teachers has no problem running up and hugging me.

Jonathan is an excellent baseball player. I'm coaching his team. I make sure at least once a weekend, even in the off-season, to run over to the ballfield and pitch to him, hit grounders, just the two of us. We'll sit and talk about school, baseball, his friends, Mom, Grammy, one on one. Hannah's not as much into sports, although we started soccer this year. I'm there for all her games. I'm going to do ice skating with her. I try to spread myself evenly between the two.

When I was growing up, we really were the family that just went to High Holiday services. I was bar mitzvahed, but beyond that, not much. My kids are getting a wonderful Jewish education at the JCC day school. I can read Hebrew, but it's a little shaky. Jonathan can close his book and say the prayers without even looking. I look down at him at synagogue and it brings me almost to tears.

As a coach I care about all the kids. I try to instill a love of the game and make sure they have fun. Some coaches are insane about winning. That's not what it's about. It's about the kids! Of course, each team will get some kids that are superstars, as well as first-time kids. I really attach myself to these kids. I made a goal that I was going to make sure that they hit the ball at least once. Some kids always strike out and it's really disheartening for them. I had one like this. In our last game I finally got him to hit the ball, and he even got to first base. His parents came up to thank me for spending so much time with him.

My company is very liberal about personal time off. I'm like Superman, I change into my baseball clothes while I'm driving the car! I drive right to the field, jump out, and grab my bucket of balls and, "Okay, here I am."

Hannah's on the soccer team. I would have signed up to be coach, but felt that you need to understand the game of soccer, which I don't. I didn't want to sign up to be coach, because there's not only my daughter on the team, but there would be 11 others. Some other parent would say legitimately, "What is this coach? He doesn't have a clue."

Even before I had children, I thought about how I wanted my children to be. Honest—because I am. To have integrity. To be a good, kind person. To have high moral values, be a hard worker. I guess I'm coming to believe that each child is actually two. The child that a parent sees at home, and then a child that everybody else sees. From teachers to friends, to friends' parents, and so on. My hope for them is that we've instilled enough in them that they believe all of those ideals, and will continue with them as they get older.

Discipline is complicated. All kids will push you. They've got to find out where their limits and boundaries are. We punish with time-outs or taking privileges away. Jonathan is getting to the age of not listening. Then I have to raise my voice and put a stop to whatever he's doing, and then he listens, because he knows at that point I'm serious.

One thing I harp on constantly is keeping their room clean. I try to make that their responsibility. You know, for example, you wear the clothes, you make them dirty, you put them in the wash. I'll clean them, I'll fold them, I'll put them in your room. They're your clothes, you hang them up. I'm not going to go and be a housekeeper, to follow around and pick up after them. I try to make them do that for themselves. I know at some point they're going to have to do it for themselves anyway, when they're on their own. I'd like them to get in that habit now. I remember my parents harping on me about cleaning up my room.

After the kids go to sleep, Jacki and I sit and watch videos of the kids. That's actually something the kids love to do themselves. We'll pop some popcorn, curl up on the couch together and we'll all watch. We'll giggle and laugh watching a tape of Jonathan running around in a diaper trying to put the basketball in the hoop. I have countless tapes!

I hope my kids get a deep love of life from me. Hannah and I went for a walk with the dog. I talked to her about everything around us, the blue sky, the trees, this earth, family, and friends. It's wonderful to be alive, and to really appreciate that. I hope that I impart that to them. I hope that because of Jacki's and my guidance, love and affection, that they pick up some of those traits. And if I've helped prepare them for that, a wonderful, happy, healthy life ahead of them like I've been fortunate to have, then I think I'll have done a pretty good job. ▪

Mike Candel, a retired sportswriter for Newsday, *is a physical education teacher and former coach for Nassau Community College. He lives in East Rockaway, New York with his wife, Mary Ellen, and has two sons and three grandsons.*

MIKE CANDEL

For most of my sons' childhood, I was a physical education teacher, a coach, and a sportswriter. Sports were omnipresent in our lives. It was through sports that I bonded with my sons. I still have this great picture in my mind of Louis at six, in the arms of Julius Irving. All the pro players knew my boy.

When my sons tried out for sports, I told them, "Do this because you want to do it. If you are doing this to make me happy, that's the wrong reason." I always asked their coaches what they expected of my kids. I wanted sports to be play for them, not work.

As a parent eventually you do give up control, unless you are willing to have a wrestling match. You learn when to discipline and pick your fights. I gave Matt curfews but he would push it. I used to bike-ride early in the morning and once caught him coming home from being out all night. So I stopped the curfew and asked that he use good judgment.

I am proud of my sons because they broke the old stereotypes. As a coach and sportswriter I often hear stereotypes about Jews. My sons were good athletes. When a kid at a frat party made an anti-Semitic comment to Matt, that kid ended up on the ground. Today there are few Jewish athletes in contact sports. If you go back to the '20s and '30s, the sons of Jewish immigrants became fine players. Today's affluent parents run interference for their kids. Parents are afraid that if a kid goes into sports their grades will suffer. Studies show that when a kid is involved in athletics their grades are better. Both my kids work on Wall Street. They work under enormous pressure, like I did during my coaching career.

After a two-hour basketball game I wouldn't want to guess what my blood pressure was. After ten years I gave it up. I wasn't stimulated by it any longer and I hated dealing with kids' disciplinary problems. At the time I had sent an op-ed piece to the *New York Times* and it was published in the Sunday edition. Then I got a job at *Newsday* doing feature sports stories. I began to have more fun.

I was in top shape and completely caught off guard when my doctor told me that I had prostate cancer. I remember my reaction to his choice of words. "Mike I have a bit of bad news." For me bad news is that the Mets lost the game. A bit of bad news is that I was caught in traffic. A bit of bad news is not that one has prostate cancer. I was so dazed that I went out of the doctor's office while he was still talking and got my wife, Mary. I needed her because I couldn't take in everything that the doctor was saying. I called her into the room because of the courageous way that she had coped with her breast cancer. Because I watched her go through it I knew it was beatable She got treatment and 20 years later we have three grandsons.

I am a different person than when I first became a father. Back then I wanted my sons to be well thought of, to succeed in school, and to represent me well. Now what really matters to me is that they find their own happiness in life.

Henry Everett, a devoted husband, father, and proud grandfather, has distinguished himself as a successful businessman and philanthropist. A native of Brooklyn, he served overseas during World War II in a combat engineer battalion. He received his MBA from the Columbia Graduate School of Business.

HENRY EVERETT

My wife, Edith, and I maintain a low-key lifestyle. We live comfortably, but have consciously tried to avoid being owned by possessions. We're pleased that our wonderful children have emulated our example.

When I graduated from business school, Jews were not welcome in finance, banking, and insurance. Given the prevailing anti-Semitism, I opted to go into a Jewish-friendly business major, retail. I became research director and economist for Abraham and Straus in Brooklyn, the most profitable department store in America at the time. My boss, Sidney Solomon, was a personal and business hero of mine. I worked at A & S for 15 years and then went into the investment business for myself. By this time, though there were still barriers, many more Jews were entering the investment business. Through hard work and good luck, I succeeded financially.

I understood as a young man that the welfare of those in need would be a lifelong concern. Philanthropic activities have played a major role in my adult life. Even when we were newly married and our resources were minimal, this realization stimulated Edith and I to establish the Everett Foundation. As success in business grew over the years, so grew the Foundation. It now funds numerous education, human rights, economic justice, environmental, and cultural programs in the United States and Israel. My wife and I have given most of our family wealth to our foundation. Through it, gratefully, we have been able to combine funding with a great deal of time and effort to not-for-profit work.

One of the important benefits of financial security for us is the freedom to speak our minds. Advocating for causes like gun control, or fighting polluters, unethical nursing home operators, firms that engage in predatory lending, and tobacco manufacturers, have been issues we have been addressing for years. We find it disappointing that the heads of many of these corporations, because they are wealthy and powerful, are often honored as "humanitarians" by not-for-profit organizations willing to tarnish themselves. It's discouraging when celebrity and wealth trump decency and honesty. It's especially upsetting that tobacco company heads have been given prominent leadership positions in the Jewish community. That individuals whose businesses are responsible for hundreds of thousands of deaths each year can be accorded honors calls into question the value systems of some our major Jewish organizations. ■

David Frum is a highly respected conservative commentator and author. A fellow of the American Enterprise Institute, he writes for the National Review, *and contributes regularly to* The New York Times *and* The Wall Street Journal. *He served as a speechwriter for President George W. Bush, contributing the phrase "axis of evil" to the political lexicon. Frum lives in Washington, D.C., with his wife, writer Danielle Crittenden Frum, and their three children.*

DAVID FRUM

The foundation on which all stable families are built is the love of the parents for each other. Mine honored each other and gave me a model of what marriage could be. Children never imitate their parents' marriages. People are different. But they showed the values and standards on which marriage was built. There was mutual respect and delight in each others' achievement.

My father's parents were immigrants to Canada. Most of my father's family was killed in Europe. His parents owned a small grocery store in Toronto, and they had many years of sacrifice. He became a successful businessman and noted art collector. My mother became the best-known broadcast journalist in Canada. To be with her was like being with a movie star and the queen rolled into one.

My parents belonged to that generation of Jews who thought that people would be Jewish no matter what, so we didn't go to synagogue very often. By the time I was 13 my formal Jewish education was over. I don't think it ever occurred to them that the day would come when continued membership in the Jewish community would become voluntary.

I made a conscious choice to study Hebrew after I graduated from college. I took on a tutor and began attending synagogue. I was in this process when I met my future wife. She became a convert after our first child was born. Our first child's

also a convert. Since then, we've become more serious. We mark the holidays. We're active members of a synagogue. The children go to Jewish day schools.

Values come from family. My theory has always been that children hear nothing you say, and see everything you do. The lessons that one learns, and the lessons that one teaches, are the lessons of the things you actually do. You try to live by the code in which you believe. If you are trying to teach your children honesty, they must see that when you bang into another car in the parking lot, that you write a note with your name and number and leave it under the windshield. That when you advocate kindness, they must see that you treat other people kindly. If you believe in courage, they must see that you do not back down from dangers and risks.

We travel a lot with the kids, and that's probably the time when we are most intensely together. My son and I were in New York last weekend. We went to see the Yankees, his heroes. After Yom Kippur, I'm going up to Montreal and I'm taking my daughter with me. We don't have a remarkable range of formal activities. Our family lives a very ordinary North American bourgeois life. We have dinner together. We play in the pool on weekends. We romp around, bicycle, play baseball. We read together. My wife always comes up with magical things for them to do.

I would say conservative values are consistent with Judaism. I don't think it's either true or wise to try to draw political conclusions from religious teachings. Religions can support wide varieties of political views, from good to bad. Oppressive political conclusions have been drawn from Judaism in both modern and ancient times. You can also draw freedom-loving political conclusions from Judaism. Religions are what people make of them. The question is, if people are committed to this tradition in the American context, what better protects and supports them? About one third of the Jewish people in the world live in Israel. They are surrounded by enemies. They have few friends. The United States is one of their few reliable friends. I think it is very much in the interest of the Jewish people that the United States be militarily supreme.

In the domestic context, American liberals often praise diversity. But diversity requires an institutional base. For example, if you have tax and education policies that make it extremely difficult for all but the very rich to afford to send their children to any school outside the public school system, you are going to smother Jewish difference. If you have education and tax policies that leave more money in people's hands and allow them to send their children to independent schools, you are going to help to preserve Jewish difference. Conservativism is a doctrine that is hospitable to religion, to independent choice, and to localism; for all of these reasons it's hospitable to Judaism. The doctrines of loving kindness taught by the prophets are not the same as the doctrines of the welfare state. You can support it if you want, but it is a creature that none of those people could ever have remotely imagined.

America has been a unique place in the history of the world for Jews. There are people who romanticize the Spanish Golden Age, people who romanticize Germany in the 19th century. Yet in the period from the founding of the German Empire until 1918, there was only one Jewish cabinet secretary. It was clear Jews were not to occupy the highest positions in society. And Jews who occupied near-high positions were victims of suspicion and rumor. There were good periods in Spain, but they were punctuated by regularly recurring massacres.

You look at 21st century America and you say, this is a special place. How can you be an American Jew and not be devoted to this country? When this country is attacked, as it was on September 11th, those Jews who are conservative, I think, rally to its defense with a more intense passion, because they are so aware of the alternatives.

My kids are huge George W. Bush fans. My son attended the first Chanukah candle lighting of the Bush presidency, not long after 9/11. It was a very subdued event, because the White House was basically closed to anybody except staff at that point. Laura Bush in particular is extremely interested in Jews and in things Jewish. It's difficult to wrestle my son into a jacket and tie and even more difficult to wrestle him into a kippah. He has one that looks like a baseball. So the president looks down, sees Nathaniel's baseball kippah, grabs him by the shoulders and says, "This is my kind of guy!" Nathaniel is not by nature a highly political person, but I suspect he'll be voting Republican at some point because in 2001 George Bush put his hands on his shoulders and said, "My kind of guy!"

My daughter's extremely political and ideological. Being in a Jewish day school, it takes a lot of nerve, but my daughter is fearless. She's very confident and has very strong opinions. Strongly held and strongly asserted! She's a normal kid, but if you live in Washington exposed to politics and meet a president who becomes a very important figure to you, your life changes. And she's had the experience of having been under fire. My kids knew Barbara Olson, who was killed on 9/11. They'd been guests at her house and she'd been kind to them and invited them to swim in her pool. For them, 9/11 was a terrifying day. It was not abstract. There was a rumor that there were sniper attacks occurring in Washington. When we were evacuated from the White House, all White House staff were ordered to remove their badges, because they were afraid there might be snipers secreted and ready to shoot.

Well, if there were terrorist teams at work in Washington, what are the obvious targets? A Jewish day school would be high on the list. They locked the school down, took all the kids away from the windows. The kids didn't know what was happening. A lot of kids in the school have parents at the Pentagon. My wife left the house and picked them up. We couldn't communicate because the phones were dead. The kids were just rigid with fear. My wife burst into tears. I made it home around 10:00 that night. We all huddled together with the dogs. Overhead you'd hear the sound of a plane and the children would sit up terrified. My wife had to say, "No, those are good planes. Those planes are protecting us."

I was not an obvious person to ask to work at the White House. I'd been a journalist who'd published critical articles about the Bush campaign. But they asked me, and when you think about it, you have to say, "Yes." I was hired to write the president's speeches on economic affairs. We assumed that the great achievement of the Bush years would be Social Security reform. I was very excited to work on that. After 9-11 it became obvious that was not going to be what the Bush administration's about. Now it's about this war. Four airplanes changed everything. Service in the White House is an honor, not a career, so when your work is done, you don't hang around. I wrote a book when I left the White House. I've just now finished another book about terrorism.

I would like my children to remember me for longevity! I would like them to remember me as somebody who lived honorably and sincerely and who always cared more about them than he did about anything else in the world.

Jay Zelinsky is the children and youth services director at the Austin, Texas Jewish Community Center. He has two children, Saida and Asher.

JAY ZELINSKY

My Dad died when he was 55 of a heart attack. He went to work one day and he died while he was washing carpets. I got called by the person at the house and they told me that they had just called EMS and that's how I found out that he had died.

In a lot of ways he was like me. At work a lot of fun, always joking, everything is great, but at home a lot more serious. My dad's life was not always easy. My dad worked very hard and he wasn't very wealthy. He worked for a rug company, washing carpets for them, and then they closed, so he started his own little carpet cleaning business, P. Zelinsky and Sons. It was a very manual job. He made enough money to take care of the family, not much beyond that.

I had two parents who tried to do the right things. They were good people that were struggling. It's hard to appreciate that or understand that when you're a kid. I think I started to appreciate that when my son, Asher, was real small. I took him to Temple, and you want them to pay attention and enjoy the service, and as I was trying to convince him of this I was thinking about things that were worrying me; about the world and my life, trying to take care of my family. I realized sitting in temple with my son that maybe my dad was thinking about something more profound than I remember. That helped me to appreciate him more.

I grew up feeling culturally very Jewish. We went to Temple on Fridays, we went to High Holidays, bar mitzvahs, we did Shabbat every Friday, we kept kosher. In the '70s, Israel was very important; there were wars, and unfortunately, that sometimes brings people together. I felt as much of a minority when I was a kid as someone who's black. I am trying to impart a spirit of tolerance and understanding in my children. I think it's real important to teach them that there are many right answers, to be tolerant and learn that other people can feel differently.

My title here is children and youth services director. We have a whole array of classes; from a papier-mâché class in art, a chess class, drama, ballet. We have an afterschool day-care program primarily for families with working parents. I have a special empathy for working parents and people who are struggling. One thing I've liked about being a director, you can create your own little world, a special unique place. Kids really need to feel safe. They need to feel cared for. You need to lift them. Tikkun olam is the theme for our summer camp this year. It's a very important value I want to impart. Helping people is very important.

I have two children, an eight year old, Asher, and a two year old, Saida. I'm amazed at the amount of energy that is required to work all day and then start all over as if you just woke up from a full night's sleep with the energy and patience that it is important to have when you're with your kids.

Saida is African-American and we've adopted her. My son is an in-vitro baby, but he's 'ours.' We tried twice to get him, so we've already paid for his college education. Parenting was a choice. We're older parents, my wife was 40 when we had Asher, I was in my middle '30s. It was something that we thought about, that we worked very hard to get. When you have in-vitro you have to go through an intense process. The mom has a lot of difficult tests. I gave her shots every day, for about 30 days. The drugs do a lot of things with the emotions of the wife. The emotion for me was wondering what's happening.

We went through birth classes. She ended up having a C-section. I was with Asher when the nurse washed him and sat with him in a rocking chair and brought him over to my wife.

I was an at-home dad for four years. I went to mommy's groups and play groups. Now I like to play catch with him. He likes to skateboard and for me to watch. He loves to take figures and create stories. He'll often tell you what your character needs to say and we'll fuss about that. He likes to have Dad there.

Our daughter is two. She's sweet, cute and real bright. She likes to climb up on the couch and jump off and laugh. She'll wrestle with Asher, she's a very sturdy kid. It's a different opportunity to have the experience of a little girl. I feel really blessed. When we adopted her, they tell you that you always end up with the kid that was meant for you. Saida is perfect for our family.

A woman connected us to an adoption agency in San Antonio, It took months to get the paperwork done. We didn't have a lot of money, so that limited us. When we went to pick up Saida, they told us this single working mom just had a baby, a single parent that couldn't afford another baby. We went to San Antonio and took the baby to the doctor with the foster parent, had a nice time, came back home. We decided we wanted to adopt her. We filled out binders full of signatures and when we were done they brought her in. We said thank you very much and drove back to Austin with her. We went to Asher's school and brought her to his class.

I think she is an amazing kid. I imagine people are attracted to her in some way because she's unusual. Nobody's ever said anything bad. She's not the norm—whether our family's not the norm or she's the only African-American kid at the preschool here, maybe, she has a pretty big personality. We had to learn how to work with her hair. She went a month ago to a hair cutting place that a lot of African-Americans use. People who we meet are very supportive. We thought about it a lot when we were going through the adoption process, reading about black history and getting more involved with the black community. Asher goes to a public school where the culture is very varied, which is very important to us.

Asher has ADHD. Some days are great, some days are harder. He talks about how some days he's fighting inside with the ADHD. It's a battle against yourself, a fight to remember all the positives that you have. They have such a good heart but the impulse control is not always there. When you have ADHD you have to go to a counselor. I want him to know it's not a crazy thing and you get a lot out of it. I can appreciate that his life is not easy. I talk with Asher about his talents. I tell him that "you are in a process," that his journey is just starting.

We do Shabbes at home. We do candles and challah and we do the motzi. We have services and talk about tzedakah. Saida knows all the lines and holds the wine glass above her head. We try to make it important, to slow down and make it special.

We've been lucky. We've never had any disasters. We've never had a smooth month where it gets really boring. That's not parenting! You work very hard at it. You get up early and get the kids ready for school, you pick them up after school and then you have the second part of your life, which is the most important. But after eight hours of work you need to take a deep breath.

I would like my kids and I to have a relationship which includes them really getting to know me as a person. I set limits at home—you gotta brush your teeth, it's a battle at times. We're working real hard to get them to do stuff and at eight years old, it's not always fun to do. I want them to grow up and have a loving relationship, that they love me even though I made them go to bed early. I've told them a lot about me, that I went to a counselor at eight years old, that I practiced saying "thank you" in a mirror as a teenager, about having to wear braces on my legs.

I hope my kids keep their sense of humor their whole life. I hope that they become educated. I hope that they are settled with someone, that they have peace in their life, that they are satisfied, that they never feel uncertain, that they don't regret too much. I hope that they have kids because I'm sure that they'll be great parents. ■

Flloyd Sobczak of Erie, Colorado is a corporate trainer and sales manager. A Jew by choice, he and his wife, Suzanne, have two children, Avery and Marisa.

FLLOYD SOBCZAK

I was always drawn to a spiritual kind of existence. I had an innate drawing toward Judaism. My Franciscan teachers never gave me the answers I was looking for. Judaism seemed to have more clarity. One of the things that drew me to Judaism was the depth of scholarship, where they wanted you to ask questions.

After college I led a nomadic existence. I worked for an artist in New York and out West for the Forest Service. I meditated and explored Zen. Then I met Suzanne, got married and started our family. She was brought up secular, but with a strong Jewish identity. With the birth of our son we decided that the kids would be raised Jewish.

Suzanne never made it a requirement that I convert. We became involved with Har Hashem Synagogue. Rabbi Bronstein kind of assumed that I was Jewish. Somebody informed her, and we began talking. I learned a bit of Talmud, a lot of Torah. When our daughter Marisa came along I wanted to be more involved. I went to the rabbi. There is a tradition where you're to reject the potential convert three times. She sat me down when I made overtures to convert and said, "I want to make you perfectly aware of what you're getting into. Anti-Semitism. Holocaust. Pogroms." She said I might run into resistance from my family and from within the Jewish community. She taught that Judaism was a grown-up religion, that it doesn't hide things. If you're willing to do that, then you're most welcome. She had very high requirements. I had to take her Derech Chaim class for eight months and to study another six months.

I had to take a 40-page test, attend services on a regular basis, get Hatafat Dam Brit, a ceremonial circumcision, because I was circumcised as a child, and then go to the mikveh.

Avery and I got involved in a Cub Scout pack. On our first overnight there was a campfire. We're supposed to put on a skit. Of all the skits on this Earth, they pick one where kids come running up yelling in a thick Yiddish accent, "The viper's coming!" Finally the last kid comes through holding a roll of toilet paper saying, "I'm the viper. Anybody vant to vipe?" It knocked me back, because these kids didn't know what they're saying and the leaders thought it's a hoot! I got kind of cranked and said, "Maybe we should try another skit?" Avery asked "What's wrong with this skit?" I told him that it's dumbing down a group of people, that it's not appropriate for the situation where we're supposed to be inclusive. Avery was just beginning to understand that not everybody liked Jewish people. Then it really hit me. I, as a father, have the responsibility to prepare my child to deal with life. How can I help him if I'm not on his side of the fence? That tipped the scales in my decision to convert. I thought, "It's time for the family to be one whole unit, that we're all in this together." I felt that in a world that can be quite hostile towards Jews I should be one with my children.

I want to learn more. I'm constantly amazed how much more there is to learn. I'm working through a volume of Talmud. I keep up with the weekly Parasha. I am very interested in study and observance, just trying to be a good Jewish man. ◾

Phil Fink is the host of the radio program Shalom America, comedian, and television performer and voice-over talent from Cleveland, Ohio. He is married and the father of two children.

PHIL FINK

I started in radio in 1963, and became a jazz DJ. In 1966 I took over a Jewish radio show from an elderly gentleman whose average listener was between 85 and death. I created an uptempo show that included interviews with stars such as Jimmy Durante, Jan Pearce, Zero Mostel, Robert Merrill, Red Skelton, Myron Cohen, Sammy Davis, Jr., Dudu Fischer, and Yitzchak Rabin. I have interviewed over 10,000 people.

For most of my career I've worked from a studio in the house. My son, Shawn, loved to help out. A friend of ours, composer George David Weiss, wrote a song for Louis Armstrong, "What A Wonderful World." There's a lyric in it "I hear babies cry, I've watched them grow. They'll learn much more than I'll never know." That is how I feel about my son. He knows more about this business than I do. At two, Shawn would sit on my lap and do commercials with me. I'd talk about one of our sponsors, a bakery, and ask questions about the products: "Shawn, when you go in there, what do they do?" He'd reply, "They give me a cookie." He was very active, but knew when the microphone was on not to say a word. He was also this way in synagogue. My wife and I have been blessed with two children that we do not have to worry about. No problems with drugs or alcohol. We always talked to them about issues and I was often at home with them. Both excelled in Hebrew school.

When my daughter, Elise, was about five, she wanted a bike. I said we would get her one. At dinner that night she said, "I want my bike now!" She marched me out the front door, down the driveway and asked, "Which way is the bike store?" I replied, "To the left" and off we went. My wife, Gale, and I were and still are very much apart of our children's lives, unlike my father who traveled three days a week for a living.

My parents' marriage was very much like a 1940s movie romance. They drove each other crazy but were deeply in love. My father was a clean freak. He washed the dishes to the point where the pots were so worn down that my mother couldn't use them. Yet, they were devoted to one another. My father died two years after my mother, on the day before her second yahrzeit. I tend to look at things with a sense of humor. So, I can see my mother calling my father, saying, "Come. It's time. This way we'll have our yahrzeit on the same day and the kids won't have to light candles twice."

My children were very devoted to their grandparents and caring for the elderly. Shawn takes his Judaism and Yiddishkeit seriously. For six years he ran a radio station at a Jewish nursing facility. My son and I follow the news very closely. After 9/11 I said Kaddish on the air. I was so choked up that I messed up some of it. I was very emotional. I was recently at a Jewish conference and interviewed victims of terror attacks in Israel. They were the hardest interviews I've ever done.

I've been on the air for many years, and have met many people who had a great impact on my life. My listeners are loyal and we have entertained four generations. ■

Russ Newman, fourth generation from Tulsa, Oklahoma, owns an aircraft charter and air ambulance company. He is active in UJA and the Jewish Community Center. Newman coaches his children's baseball teams and is teaching them to fly. He and his wife, Gail, have three daughters, Hannah, Rachel, and Tamie.

RUSS NEWMAN

A yeshiva student once asked a rabbi, "What do I do to be Jewish? The rabbi really cut to the chase. He said, "You pay the butcher in a timely manner." That's the example my dad set. If somebody needed help, he would help them. If there was a difficult issue with an employee, he'd handle it with dignity. I think of him as having "paid the butcher in a timely manner." There was never a question of where my dad spent his time. He wasn't in the bars. He wasn't chasing women. He wasn't out playing golf every Saturday. I knew what time he was going to walk in the door at night, and that consistency was important. I knew if I had an event at school, or a baseball game, he was going to be there.

My father was a pilot when I was a kid. I learned to fly when I was in high school. Flying was a common interest, a common bond.

My father was a leader in the Tulsa Jewish community. My own involvement is a product of what I learned from him. A few years back I was asked by the staff at UJA to transport Prime Minister Rabin to a conference in Washington D.C. UJA was not able to book him on a commercial flight. When I opened the trunk of the car to lift his suitcase out he said, "No, I'll do it." He was just a genuinely good man.

In the Tulsa Jewish community if you raise your hand it immediately gets recognized. Only one percent of the population is Jewish. Sometimes I am asked "Oh, how many Jews are there in Tulsa? I usually say, "Well, there's two, but I'm gone this week.

My kids are growing up in an environment different than I did. When I was growing up my family always observed the Sabbath and went to BBYO but I don't remember it being "cool." My children enjoy their Jewish learning more than I did. I feel very confident that they'll maintain some Jewish identity. My wife does a wonderful job of creating a nurturing Jewish home. The two oldest are going to Hebrew school. They all go to Jewish day camps. I flew them to camp in Georgia, and then flew in to pick them up myself.

You can really see a lot about a kid's character through the way they try to fly an airplane. Some are very tentative, and gingerly try out the controls. Others just grab and yank and bank.

It's not till you have a little girl that you realize what a society we live in. There is a lot of male domination, prejudice, and unfairness. I hope that they have the confidence and capability to do whatever they want and to do it well. I hope my daughters know that I love them unconditionally. They are my priority in life. ■

Menachem Rosensaft was born in the displaced persons camp of Bergen-Belsen, Germany to two Holocaust survivors. He has served on the United States Holocaust Memorial Council, founded the International Network of Children of Jewish Holocaust Survivors, and is president of Park Avenue Synagogue in New York. A lawyer and editor-in-chief of the Holocaust Survivors' Memoirs Project, *he and his wife, Jeanie, have one daughter, Jodi.*

MENACHEM ROSENSAFT

Upon arrival at Auschwitz-Birkenau my mother's parents, husband, and five-and-a-half-year-old child were immediately sent to the gas chambers. Eight months later her younger sister was "selected" by SS Dr. Joseph Mengele to be gassed. My mother, a dentist, spent 15 months at Birkenau where she saved the lives of many other inmates by helping them avoid selections. In November 1944, she was transferred to Bergen-Belsen in Germany, where she kept 149 Jewish children alive until their liberation by British troops.

My father managed to escape several times, once from a train bound for Auschwitz, and then again from a labor camp. The Germans recaptured him as he was on his way to obtain false papers, and brought him back to Auschwitz where he was tortured for seven months in the notorious Block 11, known as the "Death Block." From Auschwitz, he was transferred to two other camps before arriving at Bergen-Belsen less than two weeks before the liberation.

A few days after the liberation, the British appointed my mother to organize and head a group of doctors and nurses among the survivors to help care for the camp's thousands of critically ill inmates. My mother and her team of 28 doctors and 620 volunteers worked round the clock for weeks with the military doctors to save as many of the survivors as possible.

Bergen-Belsen was the largest Displaced Persons camp in

Germany. My father headed both the Jewish Committee that ran the camp and the Central Jewish Committee of Liberated Jews in the British Zone of Germany. He repeatedly clashed with the British over their refusal to recognize Jewish survivors as a separate group. My parents met in Belsen shortly after the liberation, fell in love, and married. I was born there on May 1, 1948. We lived in Switzerland from 1950 until 1958, and then settled in New York.

I grew up hearing about Belsen, and went back there several times with my parents. The first time was after my bar mitzvah. I had asked to go there as a bar mitzvah present, to see where I was born. Belsen is different from Auschwitz or Dachau in that the barracks and the actual concentration camp were burnt down completely after the war to contain multiple epidemics. All that is left are the mass graves. There was nothing physical that would evoke the horrors. I was struck by the starkness. One had to visualize within the context of the grass-covered mounds and monuments that one was walking among thousands upon thousands of dead buried anonymously.

Our daughter, Jodi, was extremely close to my mother. They always had a wonderful time together, so Jeanie and I just left them alone. We never really knew what they were talking about all that time. My mother died in 1997. The following spring I took Jodi to Poland. I showed her Warsaw and Cracow, and then we went to Auschwitz. We saw the cell where my father had been tortured. We then went to Birkenau, with its decaying barracks and the rubble of the gas chambers and crematoria. It was a grisly, gray day. Jodi and I walked through Birkenau in silence, until she turned to me and said "It's exactly like 'Dassah' (my mother) described it." I realized that a transference of memory had taken place. The stories my mother told her made such a lasting impression on her that when she first came to Birkenau it seemed familiar.

My father was the most remarkable person I ever knew. He embodied every possible quality that I would want to emulate. He was a leader. He was strong. He was a fireball. He was defiant. In his leadership of the survivors, his dedication to remembrance, to his identity as a Jew and Jewish causes, he was a role model not just of rhetoric but of action. Yet at the same time he was...my father. When I was a child, he would tell me bedtime stories, stories of the years in Belsen after the war. There was nothing morbid about them. They were about rebirth, about living. He would also be there when I had a soccer game in Switzerland, or participated in a program at my school in New York. He taught me how to swim. In fact, the ability to swim saved his life, because the first time he was deported to Auschwitz he escaped by diving out of the train into the Vistula River and was hit by three German bullets, then managed to return to the ghetto to be reunited with his father. I would sit with him listening to recordings of Chasidic melodies. I have vivid memories of him watching me from the window of our apartment while I was waiting for the school bus. I grew up admiring him for his actions, for his integrity, for his commitment, and for his ability to translate his commitment into action. If something needed to be done, he did it.

My father always wanted me to be a lawyer, but he never pressed the point. The only thing he ever insisted on was that I complete my education and have a profession. He said that is the one thing that no one can take from you. It was a matter of survival. During the summer of 1975 I told him I had decided to go to law school. He was very happy. Those were my last substantive conversations with him. He died soon after in London of a massive stroke.

I have always tried to be an example to our daughter in the way my father was to me. I learned from my father that if I could look in the mirror and face myself in the morning then my daughter would also respect me for what I was doing. The most important part of parenting, for me has always to set an example and to provide a set of values—not in the abstract, not by rhetoric, but by what I was doing. Above all, it was critical to let her make her own decisions as to what direction she wanted her life to take.

My father died in September 1975. Jodi was born in 1978, and was named for him. One of my thoughts was: how will I be able to convey to her my father and everything he represented? She will never know him. Everything I know about my grandfather I absorbed from my father. The only way Jodi would get to know my father and what he represented was from me and through me. Jewish legacy and Jewish identity can be learned intellectually, but in order to take hold, they must be part of one's being, of one's subconscious.

I have done a number of things in my life that were not calculated to make me popular. In 1988 I was part of a group of five American Jews to meet with Yasser Arafat and other PLO leaders in Stockholm. Even though that meeting resulted in the first official public recognition of Israel by the PLO, I was largely ostracized in the Jewish community, even receiving death threats. That was a difficult time for Jodi, who was only ten. She knew, however, that I did what I believed to be right. When she applied to Johns Hopkins, one of the essays she wrote was about me and that made me extremely proud. She described how she had watched me be attacked after my return from Stockholm, and wrote that the most important thing she learned from me was to speak out and act in accordance with one's principles, regardless of the consequence. I felt that if Jeanie and I had been able by word and example to instill those values in her, then we had been successful as parents.

Shortly before Jodi married Mike, a young man she met at college, they came to us and told us that Mike wanted to take on Jodi's, that is, our name. He knew how important our name was to her, what it represented, and he wanted it to live on in their children. Jodi and Mike have strong Jewish identities, keep kosher, and are deeply attached to Jewish culture and tradition. I recognize much of my father in Jodi. His spark lives on in her. ■

NEIL BLUMOFE

Music is like love. I couldn't function Jewishly without it. The word chazzan in Hebrew means visionary. The formal title of a chazzan is shaliah tzibur, the messenger of the congregation. I'm trying to speak on their behalf, to communicate with them. I respect our relationship with God. I think the narrow bridge to get there is musical. Music makes words come off the page and be part of life. Nigunim are bridges within the inner stitchings of the prayer service, making it infused with meaning.

I was fortunate to grow up in a functional family, given space to find my identity. My father taught me that the world is a complicated place and not to be simplistic. My folks pushed education but I was interested in playing music. I went to Tulane University, but I also used to play in the street. During trips to New York, I played in subways.

My parents offered to send me to Jewish camps and Israel. As a kid I wanted nothing to do with it. I thought anybody who wore a yarmulke was a freak. I'd see pious Jews walking around Chicago and feel embarrassed. A trip to Poland changed that.

In 1991, the Jewish quarter in Cracow was still in rubble. Synagogues had swastikas on them. I went to Auschwitz at 5:00 a.m. The weather was rainy and misty. I walked along the train tracks into the Birkenau death camp. I picked up a rock at the end of the track, at the site of a crematorium. I was alone in a forest, thinking "What a beautiful place," and then seeing a guard tower used for killing people. This undid me. I went back to my apartment and felt sick.

I then went to Israel and worked on a kibbutz. I went to Jerusalem to study at a yeshiva. I walked in knowing nothing, and this guy says, "What do you want to study?" I said, "Kaballah." I'm sure he thought, "You don't know your Alef Bet." He assigned me to a ba'al teshuva, a former filmmaker. I spent hours a day studying. I talked about the transformative experiences in Poland and he helped give me back my Jewish identity.

When I returned from Israel I started going to synagogue. Once while we were singing, the Rebbetzin whispered, "You're going to be a cantor." I thought about it for a year and applied to the cantorial program at the Jewish Theological Seminary in New York. While there I married and became a father. Living in New York, going to graduate school, and having kids was insane.

My son understands that in my work I sing and pray at synagogue. He also knows that it takes me away from the family a bit. I want my children to be proud of being Jewish, and also to relate to me as a father. My son was asked a couple of years ago "What does daddy do?" He answered, "He prays." He also knows that I am with people, with a minyan, with a funeral, with a wedding. I want my kids to respect and love their parents, which is a big challenge. I want them to get along in the world, but I don't want them to have rose-colored glasses about the world either.

I try to create sacred moments with my kids, but fundamentally its the everydayness of it all that makes it special.

RABBI SHMULEY BOTEACH

People always say that children are life's greatest blessing, but it's really family which is life's greatest blessing. Children are the natural outgrowth of a man's love for a woman or a woman's love for a man. A beautiful verse in Genesis says, "Therefore shall a man leave his father, leave his mother. He shall cleave unto his wife. They shall become one flesh." So they cleave unto each other, and produce a child. A child is like a river that runs forth from the spring of love, and the child cannot be detached from that spring of love. It's like a river that's no longer attached to a spring, the river will dry up. There are many kids today who are dried up. They start life cynically because their parents don't love each other, because their family has been torn asunder by divorce, because they've learned that love doesn't last. Husbands and wives need to prioritize their relationship. They must put themselves before the children if the children are to be healthy. Children need to see that Mommy and Daddy love each other, because that is going to give them hope that one day they too will find a soulmate. We empower our children by showing them that love is the great treasure of life. I try to raise my children with that example. An example that I myself lacked. I was the child of divorce.

All Judaism revolves around family and decency. Love your family and give them God and goodness, but don't limit your love to your family. Extrapolate beyond that and try to love all humanity. I'd say that that's the most central value that we impart to our kids.

Parents should take time off twice a year, go places. I say to our children, "Don't you want your father to make your mother feel like she's very special? She works hard." That makes them understand it.

I am not my children's best friend. I am their father. I don't discuss things with my kids until after they listen to me. I want them to understand why I've made certain choices. But they have to understand I am their father, I am there to protect them, to guide them, and to nurture them, and they must therefore obey me.

We eat dinner together, and after the kids finish their homework, we often have something called "Library". I take them to Barnes & Noble, they choose books, and we sit around and read. My kids see their friends the whole day at school. At night I want them to minimize conversations with friends on Instant Messenger or on AOL and to spend quality family time.

I don't think that parents regulate their children's activities sufficiently. My 14 year old, Mushkie, asked me if she could put on makeup. I said to her if it was a special occasion, like Succos or other Jewish holidays. My wife is a very wise woman. She said, "When Mushkie puts on makeup she looks 18, then people treat her like she's 18. She's not a young adult. She's a big kid." My wife was right. I went to Mushkie and explained this. We came to a fair compromise. She could put on light makeup on special occasions.

I can't stand what I see as counterfeit and artificial entertainment for kids. I hate video games. I hate television. The kids get to watch one movie a week. If they've cleaned up the house after Shabbos, they earn a video. I can't stand taking them to places like Disney World. Every summer we go camping for two weeks. I think life is a blessing and children should be filled with energy. I say to them, life is precious, don't waste time.

The whole idea of letting kids make mistakes on their own and learn from their mistakes, is a horrible way of learning. Because they scar when they make mistakes. It's such an abrogation of parental responsibility. Children never fail to ignore their parents and never fail to copy their parents.

I want my daughters to be highly educated. I don't see marrying at an early age as an impediment to an education. I'd much rather when they go to college that they have a husband. I know what goes on between men and women at college. I want my daughters to feel that they are not created by God as male entertainment. They're created by God because they have a unique femininity to contribute to the world, that it will heal and nurture the world. I want my daughters to be confident about themselves, to believe that, God-willing, one day when they date and marry, they will believe that they have something essential to contribute. They are not a man's plaything. A man should take them seriously, and treat them like ladies. Feminine dignity brings out masculine nobility.

We put all this emphasis on fathers and sons being very close, but when we go to baseball games, I take everybody. I don't believe in the whole focus on the boys to the exclusion of the girls. I think girls in many ways need more of their father's attention. I believe a father is instrumental in giving his daughters the sense of value.

We have a traditional home insofar as I'm the breadwinner. My wife works with me on everything. She is my equal partner. She takes care of the finances. My wife ultimately decides what influences will affect our children. I have to be very involved in raising my kids, but I defer to my wife's judgment when it comes to the kids. I genuinely respect my wife. I see her as my superior in every respect. I have my virtues as well, but in every area where it counts, I see her as my superior. I married above me and did that purposely. I've learned so much about goodness. She couldn't be more gracious. And that's a turn-on to me. She is one of the few people that I've ever met that doesn't have a bad bone in her body. She has a phenomenal capacity to love and to give, and she is the bedrock and the cornerstone of this family. I'm one of those husbands who truly worships his wife, who cherishes his wife.

A lot of the stuff that I write and do is inappropriate for the children at their age, whether it be a kosher textbook or the book I'm writing now about misogyny in the culture. But there are things that are very appropriate that I discuss with them. We absorb everything the kids have to say, but the kids know that their mother and father make the decisions about their lives. That's the way it should be and that's the way it is. We take pride in being responsible parents. Many parents say I want to give my kids the things that they didn't have. Hundred-dollar sneakers. The best schools. Those things are not what makes the man or makes the woman. Above all else, you want to give them two loving parents who are involved with their lives.

I'm a patriotic American, but we are purveying a very diseased culture to the world. It's a culture where women are portrayed as a man's plaything. It's a culture where money rules, and I want my children to be spiritual, and spiritually inclined.

What I learned from my father is a love for Israel. I want my kids to really love the country, even if we don't live there. Judaism is the Jewish soul and Israel is the Jewish body. It's Jewishness personified. I love the United States. I would fight for this country and I would die for this country. I love it because it's the embodiment of what the Bible tried to create as a noble society. I love this country, but even my love for America is part of my Jewishness.

I say to my kids all the time that my greatest desire is not to pass on to them my flaws, and to make them into better people than I am. I want them to have a stable household. If I show temper they'll say, "you always say it's bad to show temper," and I say "Well, I was raised in a much more volatile environment, but you, thank God, are raised with two very loving parents who are utterly involved in every aspect of your life, so you guys have absolutely no excuses."

I want my legacy to my children to be that I was a man of great decency, who believed and promoted decency, who treated all people with dignity and respect, who was always available to us, made us feel like we were special and valued and gave us a sense of significance, taught us to love God, to love our Judaism, to love the Jewish people, to love Israel, and to love all of God's children. I want to pass on a love for God to my children, and an appreciation of God's blessings. My kids are taught to love and respect all humanity, not just Jews. I love when my children learn about compassion. And being kind. And sharing. Forgiveness. Respect. I love when people say to me, "Your children treat others with such respect." That is the greatest compliment for me. I want them to internalize a sense of value, a sense of innate dignity and to possess a spark of the divine.

The need to be the man or woman who brings redemption needs to be transmuted into being a hero to your children. That's what fatherhood is about first and foremost, to be a hero to your kids. If you have impressed the whole world with your money, your status, your celebrity, but your kids don't see you as a hero, you have failed. If your kids say, "I want to be like my dad," you have been a phenomenal success in life. ■

Eric Wolf was born in Frankfurt, Germany. He arrived in New York in 1937 as a refugee from Hitler. After serving in the U.S. Army in Europe during World War II, he became an electrical engineer working on early computer applications, including Project Whirlwind at MIT's Lincoln Laboratory. Later, he was associated with the development of the ARPANET, the predecessor of the Internet. A collector of antiquarian maps and books on the history of discovery, he lives in Falls Church, Virginia with Lee, his wife of 55 years. He has two sons, Lloyd and Dean.

ERIC WOLF

Born in Vienna, my father, Josef, instilled me with a strong work ethic. I was raised to believe that emotions were not to be shown and that idleness was sinful. My home was full of books and the sound of classical music. My parents valued reading, learning, and studying as the highest achievements one can pursue, and that is how I feel today.

A sergeant in the Austrian Army during the first World War, my father was taken prisoner in the war's opening days and spent six years in Siberian prison camps. When he returned in 1920, he settled in Frankfurt and married my mother, Emilie, who worked with him in the two dry goods stores which made them prosperous. As a result, much of my upbringing was left to maids. The school I attended was the Philanthropin.

A teacher once told my father that he would serve God better if he stayed out of the synagogue; he was not religiously observant. By contrast, my mother came fron an orthodox family; I thus became exposed to the full gamut of Judaism. My mother would light Sabbbath candles and we attended Passover services, yet this made no impression on me. I believe that religion divides people and I don't like to see people with strong religious convictions in government.

In the early 1930s, I saw Hitler campaigning by car; he was a mesmerizing speaker. I know of no politician today who could match him. Had he not been against the Jews, history might have been different, but then he wouldn't have been Hitler. It is not possible to be a Hitler and be a decent human being.

After 1933, life in Germany became uncomfortable. I was harrassed and kids threatened to beat me up. Windows were smashed but our stores were left alone because we had Yugoslav citizenship inherited from my grandfather.

My bar mitzvah in 1935 was a grand affair but National Socialism (Nazism) was already rampant. It was clear that we needed to get out of Germany; I was sent to a school for Jewish children in Italy. One of my uncles left with cash hidden in his tires; the penalty for that was death.

We left Germany in 1937. Some of our relatives went to Israel, others to France, England, Australia, Sweden, and South America. We arrived in New York in March and settled in Brooklyn, next to Ebbets Field, making me an avid Dodger fan. We decided to speak only English and really adhered to that. I was told that the best way to learn the language was to see movies and I went whenever I could.

My mother died of cancer just two months after we arrived. I was holding her hand when it happened. For about a year after her death it was just my father and me.

After high school, I studied for a certificate as a radio and television repairman and this caused me to be assigned to the Signal Corps when I was drafted into the Army. When I was sent to Camp McCain, Mississippi and reported to the Duty Officer and handed him my orders, he looked at them and then asked me, "are you white?" I didn't know why he asked but said, "yes." He called his superior and had me transferred instantaneously—I had been assigned to a "colored" company. It was then that I first noticed the "colored" signs everywhere.

While in Europe, I was close to, but not at, the front lines. First it was in France where the natives were friendly and the girls welcomed us. In Germany, I helped secure quarters and supplies for our troops and did some interpreting. We reached the Buchenwald concentration camp a few days after its liberation. It was a frightful sight. I was very concerned about what had happened to members of my family but didn't find out until much later.

I came home in 1945 and started college under the G.I. Bill. It is there that I met my wife, Lee. We were married after a 3-year courtship and our first son was born three years later.

I liked taking care of my sons from the very beginning, getting up at night, walking around with them, and reading and singing to them. We took them with us on all our travels to places like the Grand Canyon, Puerto Rico, and the Caribbean. I think the joys of traveling with small children are much greater than the troubles they cause. They went to Sunday School and that was their introduction to Judaism. Except for Passover, which we still observe today, they didn't get much of it at home. I often took them to the theater and to opera. Theater is an important part of life; it's an effective escape.

My work and travels during my sons' school years were related to government business. I worked on the early use of computers to track airplanes and developed the coordinate system used to locate their position. The mathematics involved would be trivial today; back then it was not. It was part of an air defense system called SAGE which stood for Semi-Automatic Ground Environment, a program intended to defend us from attack by manned bombers from the Soviet Union. Later, I worked for the U. S. Navy and was in Vietnam during the 1968 Tet Offensive. I witnessed some atrocities and saw stacks of body bags containing American soldiers.

My basic feeling about war is that the most important thing is to avoid it. If you fail, then you must win it. During the Vietnam years, my attitude and sympathies differed from those of my sons, but we didn't talk about it much. I do remember being bothered by their appearance and long hair (I was brought up with a Prussian haircut). However, I would much rather have a son with long hair who is a decent person than one who has short hair but is not.

I have never told my sons anything explicit about how to run their lives. I think the best teaching comes out in the way one lives, acts, talks, behaves, and conducts the business of life. I did not tell them which college to attend or what careers to pursue. My father did not tell me what I should be. I went to college to get a degree that would permit me to earn a livelihood. Engineering does that. It requires math and I was always good in math.

My sons work hard and are good to their kids. They are God-fearing, not literally but actually. I am a rational creature, while religion is emotionally bound. While I may not show my emotions to the extent others do, that doesn't mean that I don't have them. I don't want to believe—I want to know. Sometimes I wish I could believe in God because it's very comforting to be able to do so, but it isn't for me. I am proud of being Jewish because of the achievements of Jews throughout the ages, and because of Judaism's emphasis on learning. ▪

Alef Bes/t: The Hebrew alphabet.

Amidah: Lit. "standing." The principal Jewish prayer.

Aliyah: (Plural *aliyot*) lit. "going up". The honor of being called up to read from the Torah scroll during services. "Making aliyah" refers to a return to Israel.

Ashkenazi: Hebrew for "German". Refers to the Jews of northern and eastern Europe.

Ba'al teshuva: Lit. "master of return" generally refers to someone who has returned to traditional practice.

Bar/Bat Mitzvah: The coming of age ceremony for boys and girls as responsible members of the Jewish community. Age thirteen for boys and twelve years and one day for girls.

Bimah: the raised dais in a synagogue's sanctuary.

Birkat HaMazon: Blessing after meals.

Bris: Circumcision.

Chai: Life; also the number eighteen.

Chasidism: A religious revival movement founded by Rabbi Israel Baal Shem Tov (the Master of the Good Name - 1700–1770) in Polish Galicia. Followers are called *Chasidim* (pious ones). Traditionally, emphasis is placed on finding God through joy and prayer.

Chazzan: Cantor *Chazzones* - cantorial music.

Challah: Usually, braided egg bread. Also, the act of taking a piece out of the dough before baking.

Chocham: sage, wise man.

Chumash: The Five Books of Moses, the first part of the Hebrew Bible.

Chuppah: Wedding canopy.

Daven: The act of prayer.

Derech Chaim: Lit. "road of life."

Eruv: A marked area of a community where special activities such as carrying are allowed on Shabbat.

Haggadah: The Passover seder prayerbook.

Hanukkah: Eight day Festival of Lights commemorating the victory of the Maccabees over the Greek Assyrians and the restoration of The Temple in Jerusalem in the second century BCE. Also spelled "Chanukah".

HaShem: Lit. "The Name". The name of God.

Kaddish: Traditional prayer recited in memory of deceased.

Ketubah: Marriage contract outlining the couple's obligations and promises.

Kiddush: Blessing over wine.

Kippah: Yarmulke; traditional skullcap worn during services or by observant Jewish males at all times.

Kitl: Ritual garment worn at weddings, funerals, and Yom Kippur.

Kosher: Food prepared in according with Jewish dietery law.

Ladino: Judeo-Spanish, the language of Sephardic Jews.

Maschiach: Messiah.

Matza(h): Unleavened bread, eaten at Passover in commemoration of the rushed exodus from Egypt, when the Israelites had to leave so quickly that their bread did not have time to rise.

Mikveh (mikvah): Ritual bath most often used by married women after menses and childbirth in order to fulfill obligations laws family purity. Male and female converts also immerse themselves in the mikveh.

Minhag: Custom.

Minyan: A quorum of ten for Jewish public prayer. Orthodox practice requires ten men, other denominations require ten Jewish adults, male or female.

Mitzvah: A biblical commandment, of which there are 613. It also means "good deed". pl. *mitzvot*

Mohel: A person who performs circumcision.

Motzi: Blessing over bread or a meal.

Naches: A special mixture of pride and pleasure, especially from the achievements of one's children.

Neshama: Soul.

Niggun: Melody. plural *"Nigunim".*

Olev hasholem: May he rest in peace.

Parasha: Torah portion.

Passover: Eight day observance of Exodus from Egypt, celebrated with a meal (seder) and the reading of the Haggadah.

Peyes: The sidecurls of some traditional boys and men, according to an interpretation of Torah that the hair of the temples of one's head should not be cut.

Pidyon haben: A ceremony performed 30 days after the birth of a firstborn male child. Traditionally, firstborn sons were expected to perform religious services for the Temple priests. They could be redeemed from service for a payment of five shekels.

Pintele Yid: A mystical concept that posits an essential difference between Jews and non-Jews.

Purim: Feast of Lots, the Festival of Esther. A carnival-like holiday commemorating the survival of the Jews of ancient Persia.

Rebbe: Rabbi.

Rosh HaShana(h): Jewish New Year.

Schmaltz: (Yiddish) Chicken fat.

Shabbat: (Hebrew) Shabbos or Shabbes (Yiddish) The seventh day of the week, a day of rest.

Seder: Lit. "order", the Passover Feast.

Sephardi(m): Jews of Spanish descent, currently generally refers to Jews of non-European origin.

Shecht: To ritually slaughter an animal.

Shema/Shma: The passage in Deuteronomy declaring God's unity, recited in daily prayer.

Shtetl: (Yiddish) Village.

Shacharit: The morning service.

Shmatte: (Yiddish) rag. The shmatte business is the garment trade.

Shul: (Yiddish) Synagogue.

Shomer: Guard. To be Shomer Shabbos means to be observant of the Sabbath.

Succah: A festive hut built for *Sukkot/Succos.*

Sukkot/Succos: The autumn harvest festival.

Simcha: A celebration or joyous occasion.

Talmud: Literally "study" - the extensive rabbinic commentaries on Jewish practice.

Tateh: (Yiddish) Father, Daddy.

Tefillin: Phylacteries; the ritual boxes (containing sections of the Torah) and leather cords worn by observant Jews during morning prayer.

Tikkun Olam: To heal or repair the world.

Torah: The first five books of the Bible, the Five Books of Moses, the Pentateuch. The central expression and doctrine of Jewish religious life and history.

Tzedakah: Charity.

Yahrzeit: (Yiddish) Anniversary of a date of death.

Yeshivah: Academy for study of Torah; religious school.

Yiches: Lineage, prestige derived from family lineage.

Yiddishkeit: (Yiddish) Judaism, Jewishness.

Yom Kippur: Day of Atonement, the holiest day of the Jewish religious calendar.

Yontev: Holiday.

Zmiros: Sabbath songs.

Library of Congress Cataloging-in-publication Data:

Jewish Fathers: A Legacy of Love / [compiled] by Paula Wolfson; photographs by Lloyd Wolf; foreword by Rabbi Harold Kushner.
p. cm.

ISBN 1-58023-204-3

1. Jewish men—United States—interviews. 2. Fathers—United States—interviews. 3. Jewish men—social conditions—20th century. 4. Jewish men—religious life—United States. 5. Fatherhood—religious aspects—Judaism. I. Wolfson, Paula. II. Wolf, Lloyd.

Printed in India

Design by Stacey Hood, Waitsfield, Vermont

Distributed in the United States and Canada by Jewish Lights Publishing, Woodstock, Vermont.

10 9 8 7 6 5 4 3 2 1

For People of All Faiths, All Backgrounds
JEWISH LIGHTS Publishing
Sunset Farm Offices, Route 4, P.O. Box 237
Woodstock, VT 05091
Tel: (802) 457-4000
Fax: (802) 457-4004

www.jewishlights.com

Developed and produced by Verve Editions, Burlington, Vermont

www.verveeditions.com